THE WEALTHY HABITS

HOW TO BUILD A RICH LIFE

AYUSH GEMINI

"To my family, for their unwavering support and encouragement throughout
this journey.

To my mentors, for their guidance and wisdom that helped shape my
understanding of wealth and financial success.

And to all those who strive to improve their financial well-being, may this book
be a valuable resource in your journey towards financial freedom."

Contents

Contents

Contents

Foreword

In this book, you will discover the habits and strategies that successful and wealthy people use to build and maintain their wealth. You will learn about the power of compound interest, the importance of budgeting and saving, and the benefits of investing in yourself and your future.

The author has done extensive research and interviewed many successful individuals to give you an inside look at their habits and mindset. You will learn how to develop a wealth-building mindset and how to put it into action through practical tips and real-life examples.

This book is not just about making money, it's about building a rich life. It's about creating financial freedom and security, so you can live the life you want. Whether you are just starting out on your wealth-building journey or looking to take your finances to the next level, this book has something for you.

The author has done an excellent job of breaking down the complex concepts of personal finance and wealth building into easy-to-understand language. This book is a must-read for anyone looking to improve their financial situation and build a rich life.

I highly recommend "The Wealthy Habits: How to Build a Rich Life" to anyone looking to take control of their finances and create a better future for themselves and their loved ones.

Atin Kumar Rastogi
Senior Procurement Specialist
The World Bank
atinras@gmail.com

Preface

Building wealth is not a mystery; it's a process. It's about developing habits and strategies that, over time, will help you to accumulate wealth. But where do you start? How do you know which habits will lead to wealth and which will hold you back?

That's where this book comes in. In "The Wealthy Habits: How to Build a Rich Life," I share the habits and strategies that successful and wealthy individuals use to build and maintain their wealth. These are habits that you can adopt and make your own, regardless of your current financial situation.

In this book, you will learn about the power of compound interest, the importance of budgeting and saving, and the benefits of investing in yourself and your future. You'll also discover how to develop a wealth-building mindset and how to put it into action through practical tips and real-life examples.

I've written this book for anyone who wants to improve their financial situation, whether you're just starting out on your wealth-building journey or you're looking to take your finances to the next level. Whether you're a student, a working professional, or a retiree, this book has something for you.

I hope this book will serve as a guide to help you on your journey to building wealth and creating a rich life.

Ayush Gemini

Acknowledgements

In writing this book, "The Wealthy Habits: How to Build a Rich Life," I would like to extend my heartfelt gratitude to all those who have helped and supported me throughout the journey.

Firstly, I would like to thank my family for their unwavering support and encouragement. Their love and support have been a constant source of motivation throughout the writing process.

I would also like to thank my friends for their support and for being a sounding board for my ideas.

I am also grateful to the experts and professionals in the field of personal finance and wealth building who have shared their knowledge and expertise with me. Their insights and perspectives have been invaluable in the creation of this book.

Finally, I would like to express my gratitude to my readers. Your support and feedback have been a driving force behind the creation of this book, and I hope it will be a valuable resource for you in your journey towards financial success.

Thank you all for being a part of this journey.

Prologue

Do you ever dream of having financial freedom? Do you ever wish you could live the life you want without worrying about money? If so, you are not alone. Many people struggle with their finances and feel trapped in their current financial situation. But what if I told you that building wealth and creating a rich life is within your reach?

The truth is, building wealth is not about luck or inheritance, it's about developing habits and strategies that, over time, will help you to accumulate wealth. In this book, I will share with you the habits and strategies that successful and wealthy individuals use to build and maintain their wealth. These are habits that you can adopt and make your own, regardless of your current financial situation.

You'll learn about the power of compound interest, the importance of budgeting and saving, and the benefits of investing in yourself and your future. You'll also discover how to develop a wealth-building mindset and how to put it into action through practical tips and real-life examples.

This book is not just about making money, it's about building a rich life. It's about creating financial freedom and security, so you can live the life you want. Whether you are just starting out on your wealth-building journey or looking to take your finances to the next level, this book has something for you.

Join me on this journey to building wealth and creating a rich life.

Ayush Gemini

CHAPTER ONE

Introduction
Understanding the Power of Wealthy Habits

The importance of developing wealthy habits

The importance of developing wealthy habits cannot be overstated when it comes to achieving financial success. Habits are the building blocks of our daily lives, and they shape our actions and decisions. Wealthy habits are the key to unlocking financial freedom and building long-term wealth.

One of the most important wealthy habits is budgeting and saving. It's essential to understand where your money is going, and to have a plan for saving and investing. By budgeting and saving, you can ensure that you're living within your means, and that you're putting money aside for the future.

Another important wealthy habit is investing. Investing is the key to building long-term wealth, and it's essential to learn about the different types of investments, their risks, and how to create a diversified investment portfolio.

Building credit and managing debt is also a key wealthy habit. Having good credit is crucial for securing loans and credit cards, and managing debt is essential for maintaining financial stability.

Creating multiple streams of income is another important wealthy habit, which can help you to diversify your income and reduce your dependence on a single source of income.

Developing a financial plan and sticking to it is also a key wealthy habit. By setting financial goals and creating a plan to achieve them, you can ensure that you're working towards a specific financial outcome, and that you're taking the necessary steps to achieve it.

multiple streams of income, and developing a financial plan and sticking to it, you can set yourself up for long-term financial success. Additionally, it's important to have the right mindset when it comes to wealth and money. This means that it's important to be conscious of negative thoughts and limiting beliefs that might hold you back, and instead cultivate positive thinking and visualization to achieve financial success.

Another wealthy habit is to educate yourself about personal finance. This can include reading books, articles and attending seminars, or taking courses on money management. The more you know about money, the better equipped you will be to make smart financial decisions.

Wealthy habits also include being mindful of your spending habits. This means being aware of impulse buying and being mindful of your shopping habits. It's also important to avoid lifestyle inflation, which is when people increase their spending as their income increases.

Another important wealthy habit is to have a long-term perspective. Building wealth takes time and it's important to be patient and not get discouraged by short-term setbacks. This means not giving in to get-rich-quick schemes and focusing on building wealth through consistent, sustainable habits.

Finally, it's important to surround yourself with positive and supportive people who will help you to achieve your financial goals. This means finding a supportive community or financial advisor, who can provide guidance and support as you work towards financial success.

The role of mindset in achieving financial success

The role of mindset in achieving financial success is crucial. Our thoughts and beliefs shape our actions and decisions, and they play a significant role in determining our financial outcomes. A positive mindset, paired with the right habits, can be the key to unlocking financial freedom and achieving long-term wealth.

One of the most important aspects of mindset when it comes to financial success is the ability to overcome limiting beliefs and negative thoughts. These limiting beliefs, such as "I'll never be able to get out of debt," or "I'm not good with money," can hold us back and prevent us from taking action towards our financial goals. Recognizing these limiting beliefs and replacing them with positive thoughts and visualization is crucial for achieving financial success.

Another important aspect of mindset is the ability to take action. Having a positive mindset is important, but it's not enough on its own. It's important to take action and make a plan to achieve your financial goals. This includes setting financial goals, creating a budget, and taking steps to invest, save and build credit.

Having a growth mindset is also crucial for achieving financial success. This means being open to learning and self-improvement. It's important to be open to learning new financial strategies and techniques, and to be willing to adapt and change your approach as needed.

Another key aspect of mindset is having a sense of discipline and self-control. This means being able to resist temptations and short-term gratification in order to achieve long-term financial goals.

Another important aspect of mindset when it comes to financial success is the ability to think big and set ambitious goals. Having a clear vision of your financial future can help you to stay motivated and focused on the long-term. It's important to set both short-term and long-term financial goals and to have a plan for achieving them.

It's also important to have a mindset of abundance rather than scarcity. This means focusing on the opportunities and possibilities available to you, rather than dwelling on limitations or the things you don't have. An abundance mindset can help you to think creatively and to come up with new solutions to financial challenges.

Another key aspect of mindset is the ability to be resilient and to handle setbacks. Building wealth takes time and there will be setbacks along the way. It's important to have the mindset to bounce back and to learn from your mistakes.

Having a mindset of gratitude can also help to achieve financial success. Being grateful for what you already have can help you to appreciate and value your current financial situation. It also helps to shift your focus from lack to abundance.

Another important aspect of mindset when it comes to financial success is the ability to delay gratification. Often, people want to achieve financial success quickly and they may fall into the trap of taking shortcuts or making impulsive decisions that can lead to short-term gains but long-term losses. Having the mindset to delay gratification and to make smart, long-term decisions can help to build sustainable wealth over time.

It's also important to have a mindset of self-reliance. Instead of relying on others or external factors to achieve financial success, it's important to take responsibility for your own financial well-being and to take action towards your goals.

Another key aspect of mindset is the ability to be open-minded. Being open-minded means being willing to explore different ways to achieve financial success, and to be willing to try new things and take risks. Being open-minded can also help you to learn from others, and to find new opportunities for growth and success.

Having a mindset of continuous improvement is also crucial for achieving financial success. This means being willing to learn and grow, and to continuously improve your financial knowledge and skills.

CHAPTER TWO

The Mindset of Wealth
How to Change the Way You Think About Money

The impact of negative thoughts and beliefs on finances

Negative thoughts and beliefs can have a detrimental impact on our finances. They can create a sense of hopelessness and helplessness, which can prevent us from taking action towards our financial goals. For example, if you have a belief that you are not good with money, you may avoid managing your finances, or you may not seek out the education or support you need to improve your financial situation. This can lead to poor financial decisions and can keep you in a cycle of debt or financial struggle.

Another negative thought and belief that can impact finances is the belief that you will never be able to get out of debt. This belief can lead to a lack of motivation and a lack of action, which can keep you in a cycle of debt. It can also lead to feelings of shame, guilt and despair which can affect your overall well-being.

Limiting beliefs such as "I'll never be able to afford that" or "I'm not financially savvy enough" can also hold us back from taking action and reaching our financial goals. These limiting beliefs can make us feel like we are trapped in our current financial situation and prevent us from seeing the opportunities and possibilities that are available to us.

Negative thoughts and beliefs can also lead to a lack of self-esteem and self-worth, which can impact our ability to negotiate salary, ask for a raise or even to invest in ourselves. It can cause us to doubt our abilities and to undervalue ourselves, leading to missed opportunities for financial growth.

It's important to recognize that negative thoughts and beliefs are not facts and they don't define us. It's essential to challenge these negative thoughts and beliefs by replacing them with positive thoughts and visualization. This helps to shift our mindset and to open ourselves up to new possibilities and opportunities. By cultivating a ositive mindset, setting clear and achievable financial goals, and taking action to improve our financial situation, we can overcome the negative thoughts and beliefs that are holding us back.

Some additional strategies for overcoming negative thoughts and beliefs include:

- Seeking out the support of a financial advisor, therapist, or coach to help you identify and overcome negative thoughts and beliefs.
- Educating yourself about personal finance and money management, which can help to build confidence and dispel myths and misconceptions about money.
- Practicing mindfulness and self-care, which can help to reduce stress and anxiety around money and can improve overall well-being.
- Surrounding yourself with supportive and positive people who can provide guidance, inspiration, and accountability as you work towards financial success.

Another strategy for overcoming negative thoughts and beliefs is to focus on gratitude and appreciate what you already have. This can help to shift your focus from lack to abundance and can help to improve your overall mindset and attitude towards money.

Another strategy is to take small steps towards your financial goals. This can help to build momentum and can help to overcome feelings of overwhelm and helplessness. By taking small and manageable steps, you can make progress towards your financial goals and build confidence in your ability to achieve them.

The role of positive thinking and visualization in achieving financial success

The role of positive thinking and visualization in achieving financial success cannot be overstated. Positive thinking and visualization are powerful tools that can help us to overcome limiting beliefs and negative thoughts, and to create a clear vision of our financial future. By cultivating a positive mindset and visualizing our financial goals, we can increase our motivation and focus, and improve our chances of achieving financial success.

Positive thinking is the act of focusing on the good in any given situation. It's a way of looking at the world through a lens of optimism and possibility. When it comes to finances, positive thinking can help us to see opportunities and to overcome obstacles.

For example, instead of thinking "I'll never be able to afford that," a positive thinker might think "What are my options for saving money or earning more?"

Visualization, on the other hand, is the act of creating a mental image of a desired outcome. This technique can be used to create a clear vision of our financial future, and to help us stay motivated and focused on our goals. For example, if your goal is to save money for a down payment on a house, you might visualize yourself signing the papers on your new home, and feel the emotions of excitement and accomplishment.

Positive thinking and visualization can be used together to achieve financial success. By visualizing our financial goals and maintaining a positive mindset, we can increase our motivation and focus, and improve our chances of achieving financial success. For example, if you want to pay off your credit card debt, you can visualize yourself with zero debt and the feeling of being financially free, and also look for ways to earn more money or to reduce your expenses in a positive way.

Positive thinking and visualization can also help to reduce stress and anxiety around money. By visualizing a positive outcome and maintaining a positive mindset, we can improve our emotional well-being and reduce feelings of hopelessness and helplessness.

positive thinking and visualization are powerful tools that can help us to overcome limiting beliefs and negative thoughts, and to achieve financial success. By cultivating a positive mindset and creating a clear vision of our financial future through visualization, we can increase our motivation and focus, and improve our chances of achieving financial success.

For example, let's say you want to save money for a down payment on a house. Using positive thinking, you can focus on your goal of owning a home and look for ways to increase your income or reduce your expenses. You can think positively about your ability to save money and the opportunities that come your way. At the same time, you can use visualization to create a clear mental image of yourself signing the papers on your new home, and feel the emotions of excitement and accomplishment. You can visualize yourself living in your dream home and the feelings of pride and security that come with homeownership. This visualization can help to keep you motivated and focused on your goal, even when faced with obstacles or setbacks.

Another example, let's say you want to pay off credit card debt. Using positive thinking, you can focus on the feeling of being financially free and look for ways to earn more money or reduce expenses. You can think positively about your ability to pay off your debt and the opportunities that come your way. Using visualization, you can create a clear mental image of yourself with zero debt and the feeling of being financially free. You can visualize yourself being able to spend money on things that you truly want or need and the feeling of relief and accomplishment. This visualization can help to keep you motivated and focused on your goal, even when faced with obstacles or setbacks.

Another example of how positive thinking and visualization can be used to achieve financial success is in the context of starting a business. Let's say you have an idea for a small business, but you're not sure if it will be successful. Using positive thinking, you can focus on the potential success of your business and look for opportunities to make it happen. You can think positively about your ability to create a successful business and the potential for growth and expansion. At the same time, you can use visualization to create a clear mental image of your business thriving, with happy customers and a steady stream of income. You can visualize yourself successfully running and growing your business, and the feelings of accomplishment and pride that come with it. This visualization can help to keep you motivated and focused on your goal, even when faced with obstacles or setbacks.

Another example is investing in stocks. If you have a long term financial goal, say for your retirement, you can use visualization to see yourself in your golden years, financially secure and enjoying the fruits of your investments. Using positive thinking, you can focus on the potential of your investments to grow and the opportunities that come with it. You can think positively about your ability to make smart investment decisions and the potential for financial success.

In both these examples, positive thinking and visualization can help to overcome limiting beliefs and negative thoughts, such as fear of failure or lack of knowledge. It can increase motivation and focus on achieving the financial goal, and improve the chances of achieving financial success.

In conclusion, positive thinking and visualization are powerful tools that can be applied to many different areas of financial success. Whether it's starting a business, paying off debt, investing, or saving for a specific goal, by cultivating a positive mindset and creating a clear vision through visualization, we can increase motivation, focus and improve our chances of achieving financial success.

Common limiting beliefs about money

There are many common limiting beliefs about money that can hold us back from achieving financial success. These limiting beliefs can be deeply ingrained and can be difficult to recognize and overcome, but understanding and challenging them is an essential step towards achieving financial freedom.

One common limiting belief is the belief that you will never have enough money. This belief can lead to a sense of scarcity and can prevent you from taking action towards your financial goals. It can make you feel like you are always living paycheck to paycheck and that you will never be able to save or invest for the future.

Another common limiting belief is the belief that you are not good with money. This belief can lead to a lack of confidence and can prevent you from taking responsibility for your finances. It can make you feel like you don't have the knowledge or skills to manage your money effectively.

Another common limiting belief is the belief that you are not worthy of financial success. This belief can stem from feelings of low self-worth and can prevent you from taking action towards your financial goals. It can make you feel like you don't deserve to be financially successful or that you are not capable of achieving financial success.

Another limiting belief is that getting rich is wrong or bad. This belief can make you feel guilty for wanting financial success and can prevent you from taking action towards your financial goals.

It is important to recognize that these limiting beliefs are not facts, they are just thoughts that we believe to be true. And they can be challenged, reframed and replaced with positive thoughts and visualization. For example, instead of thinking "I'll never have enough money," you can think "I am capable of earning more and managing my money effectively."

Another common limiting belief about money is the belief that money can't buy happiness. This belief can make people feel guilty for wanting more money, and can prevent them from pursuing financial success. It can make them believe that they are shallow or materialistic for wanting more money, and that they should be content with what they already have. However, research has shown that having enough money to live comfortably and meet our basic needs can contribute to our overall well-being and happiness.

Another limiting belief is that you cannot have money and live a fulfilling life at the same time. This belief can make people feel guilty for wanting financial success and can prevent them from pursuing their financial goals. It can make them believe that if they were truly fulfilled, they would not need money. However, having enough money can free us to pursue our passions and interests, and to live the life we truly want.

Another limiting belief is that money is the root of all evil. This belief can make people feel guilty for wanting financial success and can prevent them from taking action towards their financial goals. It can make them believe that if they were truly good people, they would not want money. However, money itself is neutral, it's how we use it that can be positive or negative.

It is important to understand that these limiting beliefs can be challenged and reframed. It's possible to have money and live a fulfilling life, it's possible to have money and be a good person, it's possible to have money and be happy. It's also important to understand that these beliefs are not facts, they are just thoughts that we believe to be true. By challenging these limiting beliefs and replacing them with positive thoughts and visualization, we can achieve financial success and live a life that is truly fulfilling.

In conclusion, common limiting beliefs about money can hold us back from achieving financial success. These limiting beliefs can be deeply ingrained and can be difficult to recognize and overcome. By recognizing these limiting beliefs, challenging them, and replacing them with positive thoughts and visualization.

Strategies for recognizing and changing limiting beliefs

Recognizing and changing limiting beliefs is an essential step towards achieving financial success. However, it can be challenging to identify and overcome these limiting beliefs, as they are often deeply ingrained in our subconscious. Here are some strategies for recognizing and changing limiting beliefs:

Journaling

Writing down your thoughts and beliefs can help you to identify limiting beliefs and patterns of negative thinking. Once you have identified a limiting belief, challenge it by asking yourself if it is true, helpful, or constructive.

Mindfulness

Practicing mindfulness can help you to become more aware of your thoughts and beliefs. By paying attention to your thoughts and feelings in the present moment, you can begin to recognize patterns of negative thinking and limiting beliefs.

Therapy or coaching

Working with a therapist or coach can help you to identify and challenge limiting beliefs. They can provide guidance, support, and accountability as you work towards changing your limiting beliefs.

Positive affirmations

Repetition of positive affirmations can help to replace limiting beliefs with positive thoughts. For example, if your limiting belief is "I will never be able to afford that," you can replace it with an affirmation like "I am capable of earning more and managing my money effectively."

Surrounding yourself with positive people

Surrounding yourself with supportive and positive people can help to provide guidance, inspiration, and accountability as you work towards changing your limiting beliefs.

Visualization

Create a clear mental image of yourself achieving your financial goals, and the feelings of accomplishment and satisfaction that come with it. This visualization can help to keep you motivated and focused on your goal, even when faced with obstacles or setbacks.

Reframing

Reframing is a technique that involves looking at a situation or belief from a different perspective. For example, if you have a limiting belief that money is the root of all evil, you can reframe it by reminding yourself that money is a neutral thing and it's how we use it that can be positive or negative. By reframing your limiting belief, you can shift your mindset and open yourself up to new possibilities.

Research and Education

Researching and educating yourself on the subject of money can help you to challenge and change limiting beliefs. For example, if you have a limiting belief that you're not good with money, reading books on personal finance or taking a course on budgeting can help you to gain the knowledge and skills you need to manage your money effectively.

Role-playing

Role-playing is a technique that involves acting out a situation or scenario in your mind. For example, if you have a limiting belief that you are not worthy of financial success, you can role-play a scenario in which you are financially successful and imagine how you would feel, how you would act, and what you would do. By role-playing, you can begin to internalize the belief that you are worthy of financial success.

Gratitude

Practicing gratitude can help to shift your focus from lack to abundance and can help to improve your overall mindset and attitude towards money. By focusing on what you already have and being thankful for it, you can change the way you think about money and open yourself up to new opportunities.

Action

Taking action towards your financial goals can help to change limiting beliefs by building momentum and proving to yourself that you can achieve financial success. For example, if you have a limiting belief that you will never be able to afford a house, you can take action by saving money for a down payment, researching mortgage options, and looking for a house to buy.

Reflection

Reflecting on your past experiences and achievements can help you to recognize and change limiting beliefs. Reflecting on your past successes can give you the confidence and motivation you need to achieve financial success in the future.

It's important to remember that changing limiting beliefs takes time and consistent effort. However, by recognizing these limiting beliefs, challenging them and replacing them with positive thoughts and visualization, we can achieve financial success.

In conclusion, Recognizing and changing limiting beliefs is an essential step towards achieving financial success. By journaling, practicing mindfulness, seeking therapy or coaching, repeating positive affirmations, surrounding yourself with positive people and visualization, we can challenge and change these limiting beliefs and achieve financial success.

Mindset practices for achieving financial success

Developing a positive and growth mindset is crucial for achieving financial success. Here are some mindset practices that can help to improve your financial situation:

Setting clear financial goals

Setting clear and specific financial goals can help to focus your efforts and provide a sense of direction. For example, instead of saying "I want to save more money," a specific financial goal would be "I want to save $10,000 in the next 12 months."

Implementing a budget

Having a budget in place can help to keep your spending in check and ensure that you are allocating your money towards your financial goals.

Implementing a savings plan

Having a savings plan in place can help to ensure that you are saving enough money to reach your financial goals.

Investing in yourself

Investing in your education and skills can help to increase your earning potential and improve your financial situation.

Keeping a positive attitude

Maintaining a positive attitude and staying motivated can help to keep you focused on your financial goals, even when faced with setbacks or obstacles.

Surrounding yourself with supportive people

Surrounding yourself with people who support and encourage you can help to provide inspiration and accountability as you work towards achieving financial success.

Seeking professional advice

Seeking professional advice from financial advisor or accountant can help to ensure that you are making the best decisions for your financial future.

Reflecting on your progress

Reflecting on your progress and learning from your mistakes can help to improve your financial situation in the long run.

Prioritizing your spending

Prioritizing your spending can help to ensure that you are allocating your money towards your most important financial goals.

Being mindful of your spending

Being mindful of your spending can help to keep your spending in check and ensure that you are not overspending on unnecessary expenses.

Practicing gratitude

Practicing gratitude can help to improve your overall mindset and attitude towards money.

Continuously learning

Continuously learning about personal finance and investing can help you to make informed decisions about your money and improve your financial situation.

Breaking the cycle of living paycheck to paycheck

Recognizing and breaking the cycle of living paycheck to paycheck is an important step towards achieving financial success. This can be done by creating an emergency fund, reducing expenses, and increasing income.

Avoiding comparison

Avoiding the comparison trap can help to prevent feelings of inadequacy and can help to keep you motivated on your own financial journey.

Embracing frugality

Embracing frugality can help to reduce expenses and increase savings, which can help to improve your financial situation.

Embracing simplicity

Embracing simplicity can help to reduce expenses and increase savings, and can also help to improve overall well-being and happiness.

Building multiple streams of income

Building multiple streams of income can help to increase income and improve financial stability.

Being mindful of your emotions

Being mindful of your emotions can help to prevent impulsive spending and can help to keep your spending in check.

Adopting a long-term perspective

Adopting a long-term perspective can help to prevent impulsive spending and can help to ensure that your spending aligns with your long-term financial goals.

Being proactive

Being proactive can help to ensure that you are taking the necessary steps to achieve your financial goals.

Being open to new opportunities

Being open to new opportunities can help to increase earning potential and improve your financial situation.

Building a support system

Building a support system can provide guidance, support, and accountability as you work towards achieving financial success.

In conclusion, having a positive and growth mindset, setting clear financial goals, implementing a budget, savings plan, investing in yourself, keeping a positive attitude, surrounding yourself with supportive people, seeking professional advice, reflecting on your progress, prioritizing your spending, being mindful of your spending, practicing gratitude and continuously learning, breaking the cycle of living paycheck to paycheck, avoiding comparison, embracing frugality, embracing simplicity, building multiple streams of income, being mindful of your emotions, adopting a long-term perspective, being proactive, being open to new opportunities and building a support system are key practices for achieving financial success. These mindset practices can help to improve your financial situation and help you to achieve your financial goals.

CHAPTER THREE

Budgeting and Saving How to Live Rich on a Budget

Understanding the importance of budgeting and saving

Budgeting and saving are crucial aspects of achieving financial success. By budgeting and saving, you can better manage your money, reduce expenses, increase savings, and achieve your financial goals.

Budgeting involves creating a plan for how to allocate your money each month. This includes identifying your income, expenses, and savings goals. By creating a budget, you can ensure that you are allocating your money towards your most important financial goals and not overspending on unnecessary expenses. Budgeting also helps to bring awareness to where your money is going, and if you are living within your means or not.

Saving involves setting aside money each month for future expenses or financial goals. This can include saving for a down payment on a house, saving for retirement, or saving for a vacation. Saving is important because it helps to ensure that you have enough money for unexpected expenses and for reaching your financial goals.

One of the key advantages of budgeting and saving is that it helps to reduce financial stress. When you have a plan in place for how to manage your money and are saving for the future, you are less likely to worry about financial insecurity or unexpected expenses. This can improve your overall well-being and happiness.

Additionally, budgeting and saving can also help to improve your credit score. When you have a budget in place and are able to consistently make payments on time, it can improve your credit score. A good credit score can open up more opportunities for borrowing money at a lower interest rate, which can save you money in the long run.

Another important aspect of budgeting and saving is that it helps to break the cycle of living paycheck to paycheck. When you have a budget in place and are saving money, you are less likely to have to rely on credit cards or loans to cover unexpected expenses.

One example of how budgeting and saving can help to achieve financial success is saving for a down payment on a house. By creating a budget, you can identify how much money you can realistically set aside each month for a down payment. Additionally, by saving a portion of your income each month, you can reach your goal of saving for a down payment much faster. For example, if you set a goal of saving $20,000 for a down payment in the next two years, and you save $833 per month, you would reach that goal in the time frame.

Another example of how budgeting and saving can help to achieve financial success is saving for retirement. By creating a budget and saving a portion of your income each month, you can ensure that you are putting enough money away for your retirement. Additionally, budgeting and saving can help you to make the most of employer-sponsored retirement plans, such as 401(k)s or IRAs, by maximizing your contributions and taking full advantage of any employer matching contributions.

Another example of how budgeting and saving can help to achieve financial success is saving for an emergency fund. An emergency fund is a savings account set aside specifically for unexpected expenses, such as a medical emergency or a job loss. By budgeting and saving a portion of your income each month, you can ensure that you have enough money set aside to cover unexpected expenses without having to rely on credit cards or loans.

Another example of how budgeting and saving can help to achieve financial success is paying off debt. By creating a budget, you can identify how much money you can realistically set aside each month to pay off debt. Additionally, by saving a portion of your income each month, you can reach your goal of paying off your debt much faster. For example, if you have a credit card debt of $10,000 and you pay $500 per month, you would pay off the debt in 20 months.

In all these examples, budgeting and saving can help to achieve financial success by providing a clear plan for how to manage your money, reduce expenses, increase savings, and reach specific financial goals in a realistic timeline. It can also help you to prioritize your financial goals, and make sure you are putting your money towards the things that are most important to you.

In conclusion, budgeting and saving are essential aspects of achieving financial success. By budgeting and saving, you can better manage your money, reduce expenses, increase savings, and achieve your financial goals. Examples of how budgeting and saving can help to achieve financial success include saving for a child's education, saving for a vacation or travel, paying off debt and many more. By budgeting and saving, you can ensure that you have enough money to cover unexpected expenses, reach your financial goals, and live the life you want.

Strategies for creating a budget and sticking to it

Creating a budget and sticking to it is an essential aspect of achieving financial success. Here are some strategies for creating a budget and sticking to it:

Identify your income and expenses

The first step in creating a budget is to identify your income and expenses. This includes identifying your fixed expenses, such as rent or mortgage, and variable expenses, such as groceries or entertainment. You can use tools like a spreadsheet or budgeting apps to track your income and expenses.

Set specific financial goals

Setting specific financial goals can help to motivate you to stick to your budget. Goals can include saving for a down payment on a house, paying off debt, or saving for retirement.

Prioritize your expenses

Once you have identified your income and expenses, it is important to prioritize your expenses. This means identifying which expenses are most important and allocating your money towards those expenses first.

Create a realistic budget

It's important to create a budget that is realistic and achievable. It's not sustainable to set a budget that is too restrictive, as it will be hard to stick to it.

Track your spending

Tracking your spending can help you to identify areas where you may be overspending. You can use budgeting apps or spreadsheets to track your spending.

Be flexible

The budget is not a rigid plan, it's a guide. You should be able to adjust it based on changes in your income or expenses. You should also be prepared for unexpected expenses.

Avoid impulse purchases

Impulse purchases can be a big budget buster. To avoid impulse purchases, make a list of what you need before you go shopping, and stick to it.

Automate your savings

Automating your savings can help to make saving easier. You can set up automatic transfers from your checking account to your savings account.

Reward yourself

Setting up a reward system for yourself can help to keep you motivated to stick to your budget. For example, if you stick to your budget for a month, you could treat yourself to something you've been wanting.

Get an accountability partner

Having an accountability partner can help to keep you motivated to stick to your budget. You can share your budget and progress with a friend or family member who can provide support and encouragement.

Review and adjust your budget regularly

Reviewing and adjusting your budget regularly is important to make sure it is still relevant and achievable. You should regularly review your budget to see if it still reflects your current income and expenses. Additionally, you should also adjust your budget as needed to make sure you are still on track to achieve your financial goals.

Use Budgeting apps or tools

There are several apps and tools available that can help you with budgeting, such as Mint, YNAB, EveryDollar, etc. These apps can help you to track your income and expenses, create a budget, and set financial goals. They can also provide helpful insights and alerts to help you stay on track with your budget.

Eliminate unnecessary expenses

Go through your budget and look for expenses that you can eliminate, such as subscriptions you don't use or memberships you don't need. This will free up more money to put towards your savings goals.

Be realistic about unexpected expenses

Emergencies happen, and it's important to be prepared for them. Make sure to include a line item for unexpected expenses in your budget and set aside money for them each month.

Use the envelope budgeting method

This method involves using physical envelopes to set aside cash for specific expenses, such as groceries or entertainment. This can help you to stick to your budget by making it harder to overspend.

In conclusion, creating a budget and sticking to it is an essential aspect of achieving financial success. By identifying your income and expenses, setting specific financial goals, prioritizing your expenses, creating a realistic budget, tracking your spending, being flexible, avoiding impulse purchases, automating your savings, rewarding yourself and getting an accountability partner, you can create a budget that works for you and achieve your financial goals.

How to save money without sacrificing your lifestyle

Saving money can often feel like a sacrifice, but it doesn't have to be. Here are some strategies for saving money without sacrificing your lifestyle:

Make a grocery list and stick to it

One of the biggest expenses for most households is food. By making a grocery list and sticking to it, you can reduce your food expenses without sacrificing your lifestyle.

Shop for sales and discounts

Take the time to shop for sales and discounts on the items you regularly purchase. You can find great deals on groceries, clothing, and other household items.

Use coupons

Coupons can help you to save money on the things you regularly buy. Look for coupons online or in the newspaper, and use them when shopping.

Cook at home

Eating out can be expensive, and by cooking at home, you can save money without sacrificing your lifestyle. It's also a great way to enjoy a home-cooked meal with your family.

Reduce your energy consumption

You can save money on your utility bills by reducing your energy consumption. This can be done by turning off lights when you leave a room, unplugging appliances when they're not in use, and using energy-efficient appliances.

Find free or low-cost entertainment

Instead of going to expensive movies or concerts, look for free or low-cost entertainment options in your area. This can include going for a hike, visiting a park, or attending a community event.

Use public transportation or carpool

Instead of driving alone, consider using public transportation or carpooling to save money on gas and car maintenance.

Shop for used items: Buying used items can help you save money without sacrificing your lifestyle. This can include buying used clothing, furniture, and appliances.

Negotiate bills and services

You can save money by negotiating bills and services. This can include negotiating your cable or internet bill, or negotiating the price of a service you frequently use.

Make a savings plan

Make a savings plan that fits your lifestyle. It could be a portion of your salary that goes into savings, or a set amount every month.

Use cashback apps

Using cashback apps like Rakuten or Dosh can help you save money on your purchases without sacrificing your lifestyle. These apps give you cashback on your purchases when you shop through their app.

Do a spending audit

Doing a spending audit can help you identify areas where you may be overspending. By understanding where your money is going, you can make adjustments and cut back on unnecessary expenses.

Find free or low-cost alternatives

Instead of spending money on expensive activities or services, look for free or low-cost alternatives. For example, instead of going to a gym, try exercising outside or finding free workout videos online.

Avoid impulse buying

Impulse buying can lead to overspending and financial stress. To avoid impulse buying, make a list of what you need before you go shopping and stick to it.

Live below your means

Living below your means can help you to save money without sacrificing your lifestyle. It means spending less than you earn and avoiding lifestyle inflation.

Get a side hustle

Having a side hustle can help you to earn extra money without sacrificing your lifestyle. You can find a side hustle that aligns with your interests and skills, such as freelancing or renting out a spare room on Airbnb.

Avoid lifestyle creep

Lifestyle creep is when your spending increases as your income increases. To avoid lifestyle creep, be mindful of your spending and make sure you're not overspending just because you can afford to.

Refinance your loans

Refinancing your loans can help you to save money on interest. By refinancing your loans, you can lower your monthly payments and save money in the long run.

Invest in yourself

Investing in yourself can help you increase your earning potential, which can lead to more money to save. Consider taking a course, attending workshops or getting a professional certification in a field that interests you, it can help you to improve your skills and increase your earning potential.

Cut subscription services

Take a look at all the subscriptions you have and cancel the ones you don't need. Subscriptions for streaming services, magazines, and other things can add up quickly and you may not even be using them.

Practice the 30-day rule

When you're tempted to buy something, wait 30 days before making the purchase. This can help you avoid impulse buys and give you time to evaluate whether the purchase is truly necessary.

Use a budgeting app

There are many apps available that can help you create a budget and track your spending. These apps can help you stay on top of your finances and make it easier to identify areas where you can cut back on spending.

Plan for big purchases

If you're planning to make a big purchase, such as a car or a home, plan for it in advance. Start saving for it early and make sure you're financially prepared before making the purchase.

Look for free alternatives

Before you pay for something, look for free alternatives. For example, instead of buying a book, you can borrow it from the library or read it online for free.

Be mindful of your spending

Be mindful of your spending and make sure you're not overspending on things you don't need. This can help you to save money without sacrificing your lifestyle.

In conclusion, there are many strategies that can help you save money without sacrificing your lifestyle. By investing in yourself, cutting subscription services, practicing the 30-day rule, using a budgeting app, planning for big purchases, looking for free alternatives and being mindful of your spending, you can save money without sacrificing the things you enjoy. Remember, saving money is a process, and it takes time and effort to develop and maintain healthy financial habits.

Tips for building an emergency fund

An emergency fund is a savings account set aside for unexpected expenses, such as a medical emergency, car repairs, or job loss. Building an emergency fund is an important step in personal finance because it can provide a safety net during difficult times. Here are some tips for building an emergency fund:

Set a savings goal

Determine how much money you want to save for emergencies and create a plan to reach that goal. A common recommendation is to save enough to cover three to six months of living expenses.

Make saving automatic

Set up automatic transfers from your checking account to your emergency fund account on a regular basis, such as every payday. This way, you won't have to remember to transfer money manually and you'll be less likely to spend it on something else.

Cut expenses

Look for ways to reduce your expenses so you can save more money. For example, you can reduce your grocery bill by meal planning, cutting out subscription services you no longer use, or finding cheaper alternatives for everyday purchases.

Increase your income

Consider taking on a part-time job or freelancing gig to bring in extra money to save. You can also sell items you no longer need or use online platforms to monetize a hobby or skill.

Use savings apps

There are many savings apps available that can help you save money automatically by rounding up your purchases to the nearest dollar and depositing the difference into your emergency fund.

Example: Let's say Jane wants to save $10,000 for her emergency fund in a year. She plans to save $833 per month. She sets up an automatic transfer to move $833 from her checking account to her savings account on the 1st of every month. She also starts a part-time job as a dog walker and makes an extra $500 a month. She also cuts her grocery bill by meal planning and using coupons. She also uses a savings app that rounds up her purchases and saves the difference. By the end of the year, she has saved $10,000 and has reached her goal.

Keep it separate

To make sure that you don't dip into your emergency fund when you don't need to, keep it in a separate account from your checking account. This will make it less convenient to access, which can help you resist the urge to spend it on something else.

Remember, an emergency fund is for unexpected events, such as a medical emergency, car repairs, or job loss. It is not meant to be used for planned expenses such as a vacation. Building an emergency fund takes time, but by setting a goal, making saving automatic, cutting expenses, increasing income, using savings apps, and keeping it separate, you can reach your goal and have peace of mind knowing that you are prepared for unexpected expenses.

Investing 101 How to Build a Solid Financial Foundation

Understanding the basics of investing

Investing is the process of allocating resources, usually money, with the expectation of generating an income or profit. Investing can help individuals grow their wealth over time and reach financial goals, such as retirement or buying a home. Here are some basics of investing to help you get started:

Understand your goals

Before you start investing, it's important to understand what you're trying to achieve. Are you investing for retirement? To save for a down payment on a house? To generate income? Knowing your goals will help you determine the right investment strategy for you.

Understand the different types of investments

There are many different types of investments, including stocks, bonds, mutual funds, exchange-traded funds (ETFs), real estate, and precious metals. Each type of investment has its own set of risks and potential rewards. Stocks, for example, can provide high returns but also come with the risk of losing money. Bonds, on the other hand, are generally considered to be less risky but also offer lower returns.

Understand the concept of risk and return

Investing always involves some level of risk, and the potential for higher returns usually comes with a higher level of risk. As an investor, you'll need to determine your risk tolerance and choose investments that align with it. For example, if you have a low risk tolerance, you may want to invest in bonds instead of stocks.

Diversify your portfolio

Diversification is the practice of spreading your money across different types of investments in order to reduce your overall risk. For example, instead of putting all your money into one stock, you could invest in a mutual fund that holds a variety of stocks from different companies and sectors.

Example: John wants to invest $10,000 for his retirement in 20 years. He understands that he has a moderate risk tolerance. He talks to a financial advisor and they decide that a diversified portfolio of 60% stocks and 40% bonds is suitable for him. They also decide that John should invest in a mix of domestic and international stocks and bonds through mutual funds and ETFs. John also sets up automatic monthly contributions to his investment account.

Be patient and disciplined

Investing is a long-term strategy, and it's important to be patient and disciplined. Avoid trying to time the market or making impulsive decisions based on short-term market fluctuations. Instead, stick to your investment plan and make regular contributions to your portfolio.

Stay informed and educated

Investing can be complex, and it's important to stay informed and educated about the different types of investments, the markets, and the economy. This will help you make informed decisions and understand the risks and potential rewards of your investments.

Start small and build gradually

Investing can seem overwhelming, especially if you're just starting out. One way to ease into it is to start small and build gradually. You can start with a small amount of money and increase your contributions over time as you become more comfortable with the process and your portfolio grows.

Consider professional management

If you're new to investing or don't have the time or expertise to manage your own portfolio, you may want to consider professional management. This can take the form of a financial advisor, a robo-advisor, or a managed fund. A professional manager can help you create a diversified portfolio, monitor your investments, and make adjustments as needed.

Understand the tax implications

Investing can have tax implications, and it's important to understand how your investments are taxed. For example, long-term capital gains on stocks are taxed at a lower rate than short-term gains. You should also be aware of the tax implications of different types of investments and consider them when creating your investment plan.

Review and adjust your portfolio regularly

Your investment goals and risk tolerance may change over time, so it's important to review and adjust your portfolio regularly to ensure it aligns with your current situation. This may involve selling some investments and buying others, or reallocating your assets among different types of investments.

Example: Sarah started investing $50 per month in a robo-advisor which is diversified across stocks, bonds and real estate investment trusts (REITs) when she was 25. She reviews her portfolio every year and adjusts it as needed. By the time she reaches 35, she realized that she has become more risk-averse, so she decides to shift some of her investments from stocks to bonds. By the time she reaches 45, her priorities have changed and she wants to invest more in real estate. She adjusts her portfolio accordingly and continues to invest regularly.

In summary, Investing is a powerful tool to help you reach your financial goals. By understanding your goals, the different types of investments, the concept of risk and return, diversifying your portfolio, being patient and disciplined, and staying informed and educated, you can make informed decisions and build a strong investment portfolio. Remember, investing involves risk and it is important to consult a financial advisor before making any investment decisions.

Different types of investments and their risks

Investing is the process of allocating resources, usually money, with the expectation of generating an income or profit. There are various types of investments available to individuals, each with its own set of risks and potential rewards. Here are some common types of investments and their associated risks:

Stocks

Stocks, also known as equities, represent ownership in a company. When you buy a stock, you own a small piece of the company and are entitled to a share of its profits. Stocks have the potential to provide high returns, but also come with the risk of losing money if the company performs poorly or the stock market as a whole declines. It also may have a higher volatility in the short-term, meaning the prices may fluctuate greatly in a short period of time.

Example: An individual buys 100 shares of XYZ company stock at $50 per share. The stock increases to $70 per share over the next year, resulting in a $2,000 gain for the investor. However, if the stock drops to $30 per share, the investor would experience a $2,000 loss.

Bonds

Bonds are loans that investors make to governments or companies. When you buy a bond, you are lending money to the issuer, who agrees to pay you back the principal plus interest over a specified period of time. Bonds are generally considered to be less risky than stocks, but also offer lower returns. They are a good option for investors who want to preserve their capital and receive a steady income.

Example: An individual buys a bond issued by a company for $1,000 with a coupon rate of 5% and a maturity date of 10 years. The bond pays $50 per year in interest. At maturity, the bond issuer will return the principal amount of $1,000 to the investor.

Mutual funds

Mutual funds are investment vehicles that pool money from multiple investors to purchase a diversified portfolio of stocks, bonds, or other securities. Mutual funds are managed by professional money managers, and provide investors with access to a diversified portfolio at a relatively low cost. However, mutual funds also come with management fees and expenses which may decrease the overall return.

Example: An individual invests $10,000 into a mutual fund that tracks the S&P 500 index. The mutual fund is diversified across 500 different companies and is managed by a professional money manager. Over the next year, the S&P 500 index increases by 10%, resulting in a $1,000 gain for the investor.

Real estate

Real estate is property consisting of land and the buildings on it. Investing in real estate can provide a steady income from rent, as well as the potential for appreciation. However, real estate investing also comes with risks such as property value fluctuations, vacancies, and repairs. Real estate also requires a significant amount of capital and may have higher transaction costs than other types of investments.

Example: An individual buys a rental property for $200,000 with a 20% down payment of $40,000. They collect $1,500 in rent per month and the property appreciates by 5% per year. After one year, the property is worth $210,000 and the investor has collected $18,000 in rent.

Precious metals

Investing in precious metals, such as gold or silver, can provide a hedge against inflation and currency fluctuations. However, precious metals can also be volatile and their value can fluctuate significantly. They also may not provide a steady income and may require storage and insurance.

Example: An individual buys 1 ounce of gold for $1,500. Over the next year, the price of gold increases to $1,800. The investor has made a profit of $300. However, if the price of gold drops to $1,200, the investor would experience a loss of $300.

There are many different types of investments available to individuals, each with its own set of risks and potential rewards. It's important to understand the different types of investments and their associated risks before making a decision. Stocks have the potential for high returns but also come with the risk of losing money. Bonds are generally considered less risky but also offer lower returns. Mutual funds provide access to a diversified portfolio at a relatively low cost, but also come with management fees and expenses. Real estate investing can provide a steady income and potential appreciation, but also comes with risks such as property value fluctuations, vacancies, and repairs. Precious metals can provide a hedge against inflation and currency fluctuations, but can also be volatile and may not provide a steady income. It is important to consult a financial advisor before making any investment decisions.

Additionally, it is important to understand the concept of asset allocation. Asset allocation is the process of dividing an investment portfolio among different asset categories, such as stocks, bonds, and cash. This can help to manage risk by spreading investments across different types of assets. A well-diversified portfolio should be allocated among stocks, bonds, real estate, and cash, in a proportion that is suitable for your risk tolerance, time horizon and financial goals.

Another important aspect of investing is understanding the concept of time horizon. Time horizon refers to the length of time over which an investment is expected to be held. Short-term investments usually have a time horizon of less than a year, while long-term investments are held for more than five years. It is important to match the investment with the appropriate time horizon, in order to align the investment's risk and return expectations with the investor's goals and risk tolerance.

Finally, it is important to be aware of the impact of inflation on your investments. Inflation is the rate at which the general level of prices for goods and services is rising, and subsequently, purchasing power is falling. As inflation rises, every dollar you own buys a smaller percentage of a good or service, so your money loses value over time. To protect against inflation, it is important to invest in assets that have the potential to grow at a rate higher than inflation.

In summary, understanding the different types of investments and their associated risks, is crucial for making informed decisions when building a portfolio. Additionally, it is important to understand the concept of asset allocation, time horizon, and inflation to make sure that your investments align with your goals, risk tolerance, and financial circumstances. It's important to consult with a financial advisor to help you determine the best investment strategy for you.

How to create a diversified investment portfolio

Creating a diversified investment portfolio is an essential step in managing risk and maximizing returns. Diversification is the process of spreading your money across different types of investments, such as stocks, bonds, real estate, and precious metals, in order to reduce your overall risk. Here are some tips for creating a diversified investment portfolio:

Understand your goals

Before you start building your portfolio, it's important to understand what you're trying to achieve. Are you investing for retirement? To save for a down payment on a house? To generate income? Knowing your goals will help you determine the right investment strategy for you.

Understand your risk tolerance

Each investor has a unique risk tolerance, which is the level of risk they are comfortable taking on. It's important to understand your risk tolerance in order to choose investments that align with it. For example, if you have a low risk tolerance, you may want to invest in bonds instead of stocks.

Allocate assets among different categories

A diversified portfolio should be allocated among different categories of assets such as stocks, bonds, cash, and real estate. A well-diversified portfolio should be allocated among different types of stocks, bonds, real estate, and cash, in a proportion that is suitable for your risk tolerance, time horizon, and financial goals.

Example: An individual wants to create a diversified portfolio with $100,000. They have a moderate risk tolerance and a long-term investment horizon. After consulting with a financial advisor, they decide to allocate their portfolio as follows: 40% in domestic stocks, 20% in international stocks, 30% in bonds, and 10% in real estate investment trusts (REITs).

Spread investments across different sectors

Spreading investments across different sectors, such as technology, healthcare, and finance, can also help to diversify your portfolio. This can help to reduce the risk of losing money if one sector performs poorly.

Example: An individual wants to invest in a diversified portfolio of stocks. They invest in a mix of technology, healthcare, and finance sectors, by investing in a technology ETF, a healthcare ETF and a finance ETF.

Consider professional management

If you're new to investing or don't have the time or expertise to manage your own portfolio, you may want to consider professional management. This can take the form of a financial advisor, a robo-advisor, or a managed fund. A professional manager can help you create a diversified portfolio, monitor your investments, and make adjustments as needed.

Review and adjust your portfolio regularly

Your investment goals and risk tolerance may change over time, so it's important to review and adjust your portfolio regularly to ensure it aligns with your current situation. This may involve selling some investments and buying others, or reallocating your assets among different types of investments.

Creating a diversified investment portfolio is an essential step in managing risk and maximizing returns. By understanding your goals, risk tolerance, allocating assets among different categories, spreading investments across different sectors and considering professional management, you can create a diversified portfolio that aligns with your financial goals. Remember to review and adjust your portfolio regularly to ensure it continues to align with your current situation. Consult a financial advisor to help you determine the best investment strategy for you.

Use dollar-cost averaging

Dollar-cost averaging is a technique that involves investing a fixed amount of money at regular intervals, regardless of the price of the investment. This can help to reduce the risk of investing a large sum of money at the wrong time, such as when prices are high. Instead, by investing a fixed amount of money at regular intervals, you will buy more units of an investment when the price is low, and fewer units when the price is high.

Example: An individual wants to invest $1,000 in a stock mutual fund. Instead of investing the entire $1,000 at once, they decide to use dollar-cost averaging and invest $100 per month for 10 months. This way, if the stock price goes up or down, they will still be investing the same amount each month and averaging out their purchase price.

Have a mix of active and passive investments

Active investments are managed by professional money managers who try to beat the market by picking stocks, bonds or other securities, while passive investments are those that track an index such as the S&P 500. A mix of active and passive investments can help to diversify your portfolio and achieve a balance between higher returns and lower costs.

Consider alternative investments

Alternative investments are investments that are not stocks, bonds, or cash. These include investments such as real estate, commodities, hedge funds, and private equity. These types of investments can provide diversification and the potential for higher returns, but also come with higher risks.

Example: An individual wants to diversify their portfolio, so they invest in a real estate investment trust (REIT) which provides them with exposure to the real estate market. They also invest in a commodity ETF which provides them with exposure to the commodities market.

In summary, creating a diversified investment portfolio is an important step in managing risk and maximizing returns. By allocating assets among different categories, spreading investments across different sectors, using dollar-cost averaging, having a mix of active and passive investments, and considering alternative investments, you can create a diversified portfolio that aligns with your financial goals. Remember to review and adjust your portfolio regularly and consult a financial advisor to help you determine the best investment strategy for you.

How to research and choose investments

Choosing the right investments for your portfolio is crucial for achieving your financial goals. Researching and selecting investments can seem daunting, especially for those new to investing, but with a little knowledge and planning, it can be a manageable task. Here are some tips for researching and choosing investments:

Understand your investment goals and risk tolerance

Before you start researching investments, it's important to understand what you're trying to achieve and how much risk you're comfortable taking on. This will help you determine the types of investments that are most suitable for your situation.

Research different types of investments

There are many different types of investments available, such as stocks, bonds, mutual funds, exchange-traded funds (ETFs), and real estate investment trusts (REITs). Research the different types of investments and understand their associated risks, returns, and characteristics.

Example: An individual wants to invest in a stock mutual fund. They research different stock mutual funds available and compare their expense ratios, past performance, and investment strategies.

Look for signs of quality

When researching investments, look for signs of quality such as a strong management team, consistent financial performance, and a solid track record. Also, be aware of any red flags such as insider trading, fraud, or lawsuits.

Example: An individual wants to invest in a stock. They research the company's financial statements, management team, and any potential legal issues. They also look for positive signals such as consistent revenue growth, a strong balance sheet and a history of paying dividends.

Diversify your portfolio

Diversification is the process of spreading your money across different types of investments to reduce your overall risk. A well-diversified portfolio should be allocated among different types of stocks, bonds, real estate, and cash, in a proportion that is suitable for your risk tolerance, time horizon, and financial goals.

Use reliable sources of information

When researching investments, use reliable sources of information such as Morningstar, Value Line, or the Securities and Exchange Commission (SEC) website. Avoid sources of information that make unrealistic or unsubstantiated claims.

Consider professional management

If you're new to investing or don't have the time or expertise to manage your own portfolio, you may want to consider professional management. This can take the form of a financial advisor, a robo-advisor, or a managed fund. A professional manager can help you research and choose investments that align with your goals and risk tolerance.

Researching and choosing investments can seem daunting, but with a little knowledge and planning, it can be a manageable task. It's important to understand your investment goals and risk tolerance, research different types of investments, look for signs of quality, diversify your portfolio, use reliable sources of information and consider professional management. Remember to consult a financial advisor to help you determine the best investment strategy for you.

Understand the concept of valuation

Valuation is the process of determining the intrinsic value of an investment. This is important because it can help you identify whether an investment is overvalued or undervalued, and whether it is a good value for the price. There are different ways to value an investment, such as by looking at its price-to-earnings ratio, price-to-book ratio, or discounted cash flow analysis.

Example: An individual is considering investing in a stock. They research the company's financial statements and compare its price-to-earnings ratio to that of its peers. They also look at the company's growth prospects and assess whether the stock is undervalued or overvalued.

Understand the concept of liquidity

Liquidity refers to the ease with which an investment can be bought or sold without affecting its price. Some investments, such as stocks and ETFs, are highly liquid, while others, such as real estate or private equity, are less liquid. Understanding the liquidity of an investment is important because it can affect how quickly you can access your money in case of an emergency.

Example: An individual is considering investing in a real estate investment trust (REIT). They research the REIT's liquidity by looking at its trading volume and the number of shares available for sale. They also consider whether the REIT's underlying properties are easy to sell and whether the REIT has a history of paying consistent dividends.

Understand the concept of tax implications

The tax implications of an investment can have a significant impact on your returns. It's important to understand the tax implications of different types of investments and how they may affect your overall portfolio.

Example: An individual is considering investing in a stock mutual fund. They research the fund's tax implications by looking at its turnover rate and the tax efficiency of the fund's underlying stocks. They also consider how the fund's dividends and capital gains will be taxed and how it will affect their overall portfolio.

In summary, researching and choosing investments is crucial for achieving your financial goals. It's important to understand your investment goals and risk tolerance, research different types of investments, look for signs of quality, diversify your portfolio, use reliable sources of information, consider professional management, understand the concept of valuation, liquidity, and tax implications. Remember to consult a financial advisor to help you determine the best investment strategy for you.

The importance of long-term investing

Long-term investing is an investment strategy that involves holding assets for an extended period of time, typically more than five years. It is a powerful tool for building wealth over time and achieving financial goals. Here are some reasons why long-term investing is important:

Time in the market is more important than timing the market. One of the biggest benefits of long-term investing is that it allows you to take advantage of the power of compounding. Compounding is the process by which an asset's earnings, from either capital gains or interest, are reinvested to generate additional earnings over time. By staying invested in the market over the long-term, you can benefit from the power of compounding, even if the market experiences short-term fluctuations.

Example: An individual invests $10,000 in a stock mutual fund that has an average annual return of 8%. After 10 years, the value of their investment would have grown to $22,851. If they had instead tried to time the market and missed out on the best 10 days, the value of their investment would have grown to $19,854.

Long-term investing helps to reduce the impact of volatility. The stock market is inherently volatile and can experience short-term fluctuations. However, over the long-term, the market tends to trend upward. By investing for the long-term, you can ride out the ups and downs of the market and avoid the temptation to sell during a market downturn.

Example: An individual invests $10,000 in a stock mutual fund. Over the course of the next 10 years, the market experiences several downturns, but the individual holds onto their investment.

At the end of the 10 years, the value of their investment has grown to $22,851.

Long-term investing allows you to take on more risk. When you're investing for the long-term, you have the luxury of time on your side. This allows you to take on more risk, which can result in higher returns. By investing in higher-risk assets such as stocks, you can achieve higher returns over the long-term, which can help you achieve your financial goals.

Example: An individual has a long-term investment horizon of 10 years and a moderate risk tolerance. They invest $10,000 in a stock mutual fund that has a higher potential for return than a bond fund. Over the 10 years, the stock fund returns an average of 8% per year, resulting in a final value of $22,851.

Long-term investing allows you to take advantage of dollar-cost averaging. Dollar-cost averaging is a technique that involves investing a fixed amount of money at regular intervals, regardless of the price of the investment. This can help to reduce the risk of investing a large sum of money at the wrong time, such as when prices are high. By investing a fixed amount of money at regular intervals, you will buy more units of an investment when the price is low, and fewer units when the price is high.

Example: An individual wants to invest $10,000 in a stock mutual fund. Instead of investing the entire $10,000 at once, they decide to use dollar-cost averaging and invest $1,000 per month for 10 months. This way, if the stock price goes up or down, they will still be investing the same amount each month and averaging out their purchase price.

CHAPTER FIVE

Building Credit and Managing Debt

Understanding the importance of credit and debt

Credit and debt are important concepts to understand when managing your finances. Credit refers to the ability to borrow money, while debt refers to the money that is borrowed. Here are some reasons why understanding credit and debt is important:

Good credit can help you secure loans and lower interest rates. Your credit score is a measure of your creditworthiness, and it's used by lenders to determine whether to approve a loan and at what interest rate. A higher credit score can lead to more favorable loan terms and lower interest rates.

Example: An individual with a credit score of 700 is able to secure a car loan with an interest rate of 4%, while an individual with a credit score of 600 is only able to secure the same loan at an interest rate of 8%.

Good credit can help you qualify for credit cards with rewards and benefits. Credit cards with rewards and benefits, such as cash back or travel rewards, are often only available to those with good credit. Additionally, credit cards with low interest rates and no annual fees are also more likely to be available to individuals with good credit.

Example: An individual with a credit score of 700 is able to qualify for a credit card with a rewards program and a 0% introductory interest rate. An individual with a credit score of 600 is only able to qualify for a credit card with a higher interest rate and no rewards program.

Good credit can help you in other areas of your life. Good credit can also have an impact on other areas of your life such as renting an apartment, getting a job, or even getting a cell phone plan. Landlords and employers may check your credit score as part of their decision-making process.

Understanding debt can help you manage it effectively. Knowing how much debt you have and how it's spread out between different types of loans can help you prioritize which debts to pay off first and develop a plan to pay them off in a timely manner.

Example: An individual has credit card debt, student loan debt, and car loan debt. They prioritize paying off the credit card debt first because it has the highest interest rate and can have the greatest impact on their credit score.

Understanding debt can help you avoid financial trouble. It's important to be aware of your debt-to-income ratio and make sure you're not taking on too much debt. If you're unable to make your debt payments, it can lead to late fees, penalties, and damage to your credit score.

Understanding the difference between good and bad debt. Not all debt is bad, some types of debt, such as a mortgage or student loan, can help you achieve long-term goals and investments. However, credit card debt and personal loans can be considered as bad debt as it usually used for non-essential and non-investment purposes. Understanding the difference between good and bad debt can help you make better financial decisions and prioritize which debts to pay off first.

Example: An individual has a mortgage and a student loan, which are considered as good debt because they are used to purchase a home and finance education, respectively. They also have credit card debt and personal loan, which are considered as bad debt as they were used for non-essential and non-investment purposes. They prioritize paying off the credit card debt and personal loan first because they have higher interest rates and can have a greater impact on their credit score.

Understanding credit utilization and its impact on credit score. Credit utilization is the amount of credit you are using compared to the amount of credit available to you. High credit utilization can negatively impact your credit score, as it can indicate to lenders that you are relying too heavily on credit. Keeping your credit utilization low by paying off debt or increasing your credit limit can help to improve your credit score.

Example: An individual has a credit card with a limit of $10,000 and a balance of $5,000. Their credit utilization is 50%. They pay off $2,500 of their balance and their credit utilization is now 25%. This can have a positive impact on their credit score and make them appear more financially responsible to lenders.

In conclusion, understanding credit and debt is important for managing your finances. Good credit can help you secure loans and lower interest rates, qualify for credit cards with rewards and benefits, and help you in other areas of your life. Understanding debt can help you manage it effectively and avoid financial trouble.Knowing the difference between good and bad debt, the impact of credit utilization on credit score and how to prioritize your debts can help you achieve your financial goals and avoid financial trouble. Consult a financial advisor to help you determine the best strategy for managing your credit and debt.

How to build good credit

Building good credit is an important step in achieving financial stability and independence. A good credit score can make it easier to secure loans, qualify for credit cards with rewards and benefits, and even help you in other areas of your life, such as renting an apartment or getting a job. Here are some tips on how to build good credit:

Make sure you are on the electoral roll

This will help to confirm your identity and address, and make it easier for lenders to verify your information when you apply for credit.

Example: An individual is not on the electoral roll and applies for a credit card. The lender is unable to verify their identity and address, so the application is denied. The individual registers to vote and applies for the credit card again. This time, the lender is able to verify their identity and address, and the application is approved.

Get a credit card

Having a credit card is one of the easiest ways to start building your credit history. Just make sure to use it responsibly and pay your bill on time every month.

Example: An individual gets a credit card and uses it to make small purchases every month. They pay their bill on time and in

full every month. This responsible use of credit helps to improve
their credit score.

Keep credit card balances low

High credit card balances can indicate to lenders that you are
relying too heavily on credit and can negatively impact your credit
score. Try to keep your credit card balances low, ideally under
30% of your credit limit.

Example: An individual has a credit card with a limit of $1,000.
They have a balance of $700. This is a high credit utilization rate
of 70%. They pay off $500 of their balance and their credit
utilization rate is now 35%. This can have a positive impact on
their credit score.

Diversify your credit

Having different types of credit, such as a credit card and a loan,
can help to improve your credit score. This is because it shows
lenders that you can handle different types of credit responsibly.

Example: An individual has a credit card and a car loan. This
shows lenders that they can handle different types of credit
responsibly and can help to improve their credit score.

Monitor your credit report

It's important to check your credit report regularly to make sure that all the information on it is accurate. If you notice any errors, contact the credit bureau and the lender to have them corrected.

Example: An individual checks their credit report and notices that there is an error on it. They contact the credit bureau and the lender to have the error corrected. This can help to improve their credit score.

Pay your bills on time

Late payments can have a negative impact on your credit score and can stay on your credit report for up to seven years. Set up automatic payments or reminders to ensure that you pay your bills on time every month.

Example: An individual sets up automatic payments for their credit card and loan payments. They never miss a payment and their credit score improves as a result.

Keep old credit accounts open

Closing an old credit account can shorten your credit history, which can negatively impact your credit score. Keeping old credit accounts open, even if you're not using them, can help to improve your credit score by showing a longer credit history.

Example: An individual closes a credit card account they've had for 10 years. This shortens their credit history and can have a negative impact on their credit score. They decide to keep the account open and their credit score improves.

Avoid applying for too much credit at once

Each time you apply for credit, it generates a hard inquiry on your credit report, which can have a negative impact on your credit score. Try to avoid applying for too much credit at once and space out your applications over time.

Example: An individual applies for several credit cards and loans at once. This generates several hard inquiries on their credit report and can have a negative impact on their credit score. They decide to space out their credit applications over time and their credit score improves.

Have a positive payment history

Your payment history is one of the most important factors in determining your credit score. The longer your positive payment history, the better your credit score will be.

Example: An individual has a long positive payment history of paying their bills on time. This helps to improve their credit score over time.

Building good credit takes time and discipline

It's important to be aware of the different factors that can impact your credit score and to take steps to improve it. Remember to consult a financial advisor to help you determine the best strategy for building good credit.

Be mindful of your credit utilization

Credit utilization, or the amount of credit you are using compared to the amount of credit available to you, is one of the most important factors in determining your credit score. Keep your credit utilization low, ideally under 30% of your credit limit, to help improve your credit score.

Example: An individual has a credit card with a limit of $5,000 and a balance of $2,500. Their credit utilization is 50%. They pay off $500 of their balance and their credit utilization is now 20%. This can have a positive impact on their credit score.

Use a secured credit card

A secured credit card is a type of credit card that requires a security deposit before it can be used. It is an excellent option for people who are trying to build or rebuild their credit. Using a secured credit card responsibly can help to improve your credit score.

Example: An individual has no credit history and wants to build credit. They decide to open a secured credit card and deposit $500 as a security deposit. They use the card responsibly and make payments on time. Over time, their credit score improves.

Be aware of the Credit Mix

The credit mix is the different types of credit you have, such as credit cards, car loans, mortgages and personal loans. Having a diverse credit mix can help to improve your credit score.

Example: An individual has a credit card and a car loan. This shows lenders that they can handle different types of credit responsibly, and it can help to improve their credit score.

Limit the number of credit applications

Every time you apply for credit, it generates a hard inquiry on your credit report, which can have a negative impact on your credit score. Try to limit the number of credit applications you make and space them out over time.

Example: An individual applies for several credit cards and loans at once. This generates several hard inquiries on their credit report and can have a negative impact on their credit score. They decide to space out their credit applications over time and their credit score improves.

In conclusion, building good credit takes time and discipline, but the effort is worth it. By being mindful of your credit utilization, using a secured credit card, be aware of the Credit Mix, limiting the number of credit applications, paying your bills on time, keeping old credit accounts open, avoiding applying for too much credit at once, having a positive payment history, and monitoring your credit report regularly, you can improve your credit score and achieve your financial goals. Remember to consult a financial advisor to help you determine the best strategy for building good credit.

Strategies for managing and paying off debt

Managing and paying off debt can be a difficult task, but with the right strategies, it's possible to become debt-free and achieve financial stability. Here are some strategies for managing and paying off debt:

Create a budget

Creating a budget is the first step in managing your debt. It will help you understand where your money is going and identify areas where you can cut back in order to put more money towards paying off your debt.

Example: An individual creates a budget and realizes they are spending a lot of money on eating out. They decide to cut back on eating out and put the money they save towards paying off their credit card debt.

Prioritize your debts

Not all debts are created equal, some have higher interest rates than others. Prioritizing your debts by paying off the ones with the highest interest rates first can help you save money in the long run.

Example: An individual has credit card debt with an interest rate of 20% and a car loan with an interest rate of 4%. They prioritize paying off the credit card debt first because the interest rate is higher and it can have a greater impact on their credit score.

Use the snowball method or the avalanche method

The snowball method involves paying off your smallest debt first, while the avalanche method involves paying off your highest interest rate debt first. Both methods can be effective, and it's important to choose the one that works best for you and your financial situation.

Example: An individual uses the snowball method and pays off their smallest debt first. This helps them to see progress and stay motivated to continue paying off their debts.

Consolidate your debt

Consolidating your debt can make it easier to manage by combining multiple debts into one monthly payment. This can also help to reduce the overall interest rate and save money in the long run.

Example: An individual consolidates their credit card debt, personal loan and car loan into one monthly payment. This makes it easier for them to manage their debt and they also save money in the long run by reducing the overall interest rate.

Consider professional help

If your debt is overwhelming and you're finding it difficult to manage, consider seeking professional help from a financial advisor or credit counselor. They can help you create a debt management plan and negotiate with creditors on your behalf.

Example: An individual seeks professional help from a financial advisor. The advisor helps them to create a debt management plan and negotiate with creditors to lower their interest rates. This helps them to pay off their debt faster and save money in the long run.

Use the extra money wisely

Once you have a plan in place to pay off your debt, it's important to use any extra money you have wisely. Instead of using it to buy unnecessary things or to increase your lifestyle, you should use it to pay off your debt. This will help you reach your goal faster.

Example: An individual receives a bonus at work. Instead of using it to buy a new TV, they decide to use it to pay off a portion of their credit card debt. This helps them to reach their goal of becoming debt-free faster.

Avoid new debt

While you are working on paying off your debt, it's important to avoid taking on new debt. This means avoiding using your credit cards and not taking out any new loans. This will help you to stay focused on your goal and not add more debt to your plate.

Example: An individual is working on paying off their credit card debt. They avoid using their credit cards and are not taking out any new loans. This helps them to stay focused on their goal and not add more debt to their plate.

Keep yourself motivated

Paying off debt can be a long and difficult process. It's important to keep yourself motivated by setting achievable short-term goals, reminding yourself why you started and celebrating small wins along the way.

Example: An individual sets a goal to pay off $5,000 of their credit card debt in 6 months. They track their progress and celebrate small wins along the way. This helps them to stay motivated and reach their goal.

Learn from your mistakes

If you have accumulated debt, it's important to learn from your mistakes and understand what led you to that point. This will help you to make better financial decisions in the future and avoid falling into debt again.

Consider a balance transfer

A balance transfer can be a useful tool for managing and paying off debt. It allows you to transfer high-interest credit card debt to a card with a lower interest rate. This can help you save money on interest and pay off your debt faster.

Example: An individual has credit card debt with an interest rate of 20%. They transfer their balance to a card with an interest rate of 12%. This helps them to save money on interest and pay off their debt faster.

Take advantage of debt forgiveness programs

Some debts, such as student loans, may have forgiveness programs available. Make sure to research and take advantage of any forgiveness programs that may be available to you.

Example: An individual has student loan debt. They research and find out that there is a forgiveness program available for public service employees. They qualify for the program and have a portion of their debt forgiven.

Negotiate with creditors

If you're having trouble making your payments, don't be afraid to reach out to your creditors and negotiate a payment plan that works for both parties. This can help to prevent late payments and potential defaults on your loans.

Example: An individual is having trouble making their car loan payments. They reach out to the lender and negotiate a new payment plan with lower monthly payments. This helps them to avoid defaulting on the loan.

In conclusion, managing and paying off debt requires a solid plan, discipline, and patience. By creating a budget, prioritizing your debts, using the snowball or avalanche method, consolidating your debt, seeking professional help, using extra money wisely, avoiding new debt, keeping yourself motivated, learning from your mistakes, considering a balance transfer, taking advantage of debt forgiveness programs, and negotiating with creditors, you can become debt-free and achieve financial stability. Remember to consult a financial advisor to help you determine the best strategy for managing and paying off your debt.

How to avoid common debt traps

Debt can be a difficult thing to manage and can often lead to more debt if not handled properly. Here are some common debt traps and how to avoid them:

Minimum payments trap

Many credit card companies only require a minimum payment, which can lead to paying only the interest and not making a dent in the principal balance. To avoid this trap, pay more than the minimum payment each month.

Example: An individual has a credit card balance of $5,000 with a minimum payment of $100. If they only make the minimum payment, it will take them over 20 years to pay off the debt and they will end up paying over $8,000 in interest. To avoid this trap, they decide to pay $200 per month and pay off the debt in 3 years and pay $1,800 in interest.

Debt consolidation trap

Consolidating your debt can seem like a good idea, but it can lead to more debt if you don't address the underlying issues that caused the debt in the first place. To avoid this trap, make sure to create a budget, stick to it and address the underlying issues that caused the debt.

Example: An individual consolidates their credit card debt, personal loan and car loan into one monthly payment. But they don't address the underlying issues that caused the debt such as overspending and not keeping track of their finances. As a result, they end up accumulating more debt. To avoid this trap, they create a budget, stick to it and address the underlying issues that caused the debt.

Refinancing trap

Refinancing can seem like a good idea, but it can lead to more debt if you don't understand the terms and end up with a higher interest rate or longer loan term. To avoid this trap, make sure to understand the terms of the loan, shop around for the best rates and only refinance if it will save you money in the long run.

Example: An individual refinances their car loan to lower their monthly payments. But they don't understand the terms and end up with a longer loan term and a higher interest rate. As a result, they end up paying more in interest over the life of the loan. To avoid this trap, they shop around for the best rates and only refinance if it will save them money in the long run.

Balance transfer trap

Balance transfers can seem like a good idea, but they can lead to more debt if you don't pay off the transferred balance before the introductory rate expires. To avoid this trap, make sure to pay off the transferred balance before the introductory rate expires and avoid using the transferred balance to make new purchases.

Example: An individual does a balance transfer to a credit card with a 0% intro APR. But they don't pay off the transferred balance before the introductory rate expires, and they end up with a higher interest rate. To avoid this trap, they make a plan to pay off the transferred balance before the introductory rate expires and avoid using the transferred balance to make new purchases.

Payday loan trap

Payday loans can seem like an easy way to get money quickly, but they can lead to more debt with high-interest rates and short-term repayment periods. To avoid this trap, avoid taking out payday loans, and instead, look for alternative options such as personal loans with lower interest rates and longer repayment periods.

Example: An individual takes out a payday loan to cover unexpected expenses. But they can't pay it back on the due date, they end up taking out more loans to pay off the original loan, and they end up with a cycle of debt. To avoid this trap, they look for alternative options such as a personal loan with a lower interest rate and a longer repayment period.

In conclusion, it is important to be aware of common debt traps, such as minimum payments trap, debt consolidation trap, refinancing trap, balance transfer trap, and payday loan trap. By creating a budget, understanding the terms of loans, avoiding new debt, and seeking alternative options, you can avoid falling into these traps and work towards becoming debt-free. Remember to consult a financial advisor to help you determine the best strategy for avoiding common debt traps and managing your debt

Building Multiple Streams of Income

Understanding the importance of diversifying your income

Diversifying your income is important for achieving financial stability and achieving your financial goals. By having multiple streams of income, you can reduce your dependence on a single source of income, which can help to mitigate financial risks and provide a cushion against unexpected events such as job loss or a downturn in the economy. Here are some ways to diversify your income and the benefits of doing so:

Invest in real estate

One way to diversify your income is to invest in real estate. This can include buying rental properties, becoming a landlord, or flipping houses. The benefit of this is that real estate can provide a steady stream of passive income in the form of rent. Additionally, real estate can also appreciate in value over time, providing the potential for capital gains.

Example: An individual decides to invest in a rental property. They purchase a property for $200,000 and rent it out for $1,500 per month. This provides a steady stream of passive income in the form of rent and the potential for capital gains as the property appreciates in value over time.

Start a side hustle

Another way to diversify your income is to start a side hustle. This can include starting a business, freelancing, or providing consulting services. The benefit of this is that it can provide an additional stream of income and also give you the opportunity to pursue your passions and interests.

Example: An individual decides to start a side hustle as a freelance graphic designer. They work on projects for clients on the weekends and make an additional $500 per month. This provides an additional stream of income and allows them to pursue their passion for design.

Invest in stocks or bonds

Investing in stocks or bonds can provide a diversified stream of income in the form of dividends or interest. The benefit of this is that it can provide a steady stream of income, and there is also the potential for capital gains as the value of the investments increases.

Example: An individual decides to invest $10,000 in a stock that pays dividends of 4%. This provides a steady stream of income in the form of dividends and the potential for capital gains as the value of the stock increases.

Save for retirement

Another way to diversify your income is to save for retirement. This can include contributing to a 401(k) or IRA, and the benefit of this is that it can provide a steady stream of income in the form of pension or social security benefits.

Example: An individual starts contributing to their 401(k) at age 25 and retires at age 65. By the time they retire, their 401(k) balance is worth $500,000 and provides a steady stream of income in the form of pension or social security benefits.

Create digital products or online courses

Creating digital products or online courses can provide a diversified stream of income through online sales. The benefit of this is that it can provide a passive income stream and also allows you to share your knowledge and expertise with others.

Example: An individual creates an online course on how to start a business. They market the course and make sales, earning a passive stream of income while also sharing their expertise with others.

Participate in affiliate marketing

Affiliate marketing is a performance-based marketing in which a business rewards one or more affiliates for each visitor or customer brought about by the affiliate's own marketing efforts. The benefit of this is that it can provide an additional stream of income with minimal effort and also allows you to promote products or services that align with your interests.

Example: An individual participates in affiliate marketing by promoting a book on personal finance on their blog. They include an affiliate link to the book and earn a commission for each sale made through the link, providing an additional stream of income.

Rent out a spare room or storage space

If you have extra space in your home, such as a spare room or storage space, you can rent it out to provide an additional stream of income. The benefit of this is that it can provide a passive income stream with minimal effort and also allows you to utilize the space you already have.

Example: An individual rents out a spare room on Airbnb, providing an additional stream of income while also allowing them to utilize the space they already have.

Offer a paid service or subscription

If you have a skill or expertise that others are willing to pay for, you can offer a paid service or subscription to provide an additional stream of income. The benefit of this is that it allows you to monetize your skills and expertise and also provides a recurring income stream.

Example: An individual offers a paid subscription service for personalized meal planning and nutrition coaching, providing an additional stream of income while also allowing them to monetize their skills and expertise as a nutritionist.

In conclusion, diversifying your income is important for achieving financial stability and achieving your financial goals. By creating multiple streams of income, you can reduce your dependence on a single source of income, which can help to mitigate financial risks and provide a cushion against unexpected events such as job loss or a downturn in the economy. Remember to consult a financial advisor to help you determine the best strategy for diversifying

your income and to ensure that it aligns with your overall
financial plan.

How to create multiple streams of income

Creating multiple streams of income is a key strategy for achieving financial stability and reaching your financial goals. By having more than one source of income, you can reduce your dependence on a single source of income and mitigate financial risks. Here are some ways to create multiple streams of income and the benefits of doing so:

Start a side business

One way to create multiple streams of income is to start a side business. This can include starting a small business, becoming a freelancer, or providing consulting services. The benefit of this is that it can provide an additional stream of income and also give you the opportunity to pursue your passions and interests.

Example: An individual starts a side business as a freelance graphic designer. They work on projects for clients on the weekends and make an additional $500 per month. This provides an additional stream of income and allows them to pursue their passion for design.

Invest in stocks or bonds

Investing in stocks or bonds can provide a diversified stream of income in the form of dividends or interest. The benefit of this is that it can provide a steady stream of income, and there is also the potential for capital gains as the value of the investments increases.

Example: An individual decides to invest $10,000 in a stock that pays dividends of 4%. This provides a steady stream of income in the form of dividends and the potential for capital gains as the value of the stock increases.

Rent out a spare room or storage space

If you have extra space in your home, such as a spare room or storage space, you can rent it out to provide an additional stream of income. The benefit of this is that it can provide a passive income stream with minimal effort and also allows you to utilize the space you already have.

Example: An individual rents out a spare room on Airbnb, providing an additional stream of income while also allowing them to utilize the space they already have.

Create digital products or online courses

Creating digital products or online courses can provide a diversified stream of income through online sales. The benefit of this is that it can provide a passive income stream and also allows you to share your knowledge and expertise with others.

Example: An individual creates an online course on how to start a business. They market the course and make sales, earning a passive stream of income while also sharing their expertise with others.

Participate in affiliate marketing

Affiliate marketing is a performance-based marketing in which a business rewards one or more affiliates for each visitor or customer brought about by the affiliate's own marketing efforts. The benefit of this is that it can provide an additional stream of income with minimal effort and also allows you to promote products or services that align with your interests.

Example: An individual participates in affiliate marketing by promoting a book on personal finance on their blog. They include an affiliate link to the book and earn a commission for each sale made through the link, providing an additional stream of income.

Start a blog or a website

Starting a blog or a website can provide multiple streams of income through advertising, sponsored content, and affiliate marketing. The benefit of this is that it allows you to share your knowledge and expertise with others and also provides an opportunity to monetize your content and audience.

Example: An individual starts a blog about personal finance and earns money through advertising, sponsored content, and affiliate marketing. They also have the opportunity to monetize their audience by selling e-books, courses or consulting services.

Offer a paid service or subscription

If you have a skill or expertise that others are willing to pay for, you can offer a paid service or subscription to provide an additional stream of income. The benefit of this is that it allows you to monetize your skills and expertise and also provides a recurring income stream.

Example: An individual offers a paid subscription service for personalized meal planning and nutrition coaching, providing an additional stream of income while also allowing them to monetize their skills and expertise as a nutritionist.

Participate in the sharing economy

The sharing economy is a system where people can lend or borrow goods or services from each other. The benefit of this is that it allows you to monetize resources that you already own and also provides an additional stream of income.

Example: An individual rents out their car on Turo when they are not using it, providing an additional stream of income while also allowing them to monetize a resource they already own.

Creating multiple streams of income is a key strategy for achieving financial stability and reaching your financial goals. By starting a side business, investing in stocks or bonds, renting out a spare room or storage space, creating digital products or online courses, participating in affiliate marketing, starting a blog or website, offering a paid service or subscription, participating in the sharing economy, and so on, you can reduce your dependence on a single source of income and mitigate financial risks. Remember, the key is to identify your interests, skills, and resources, and then find ways to monetize them. It is important to have a well-rounded approach, and not to put all your eggs in one basket. Additionally, it is essential to consult a financial advisor to help you determine the best strategy for creating multiple streams of income and to ensure that it aligns with your overall financial plan.

Save for retirement

Another way to create multiple streams of income is to save for retirement. This can include contributing to a 401(k) or IRA, and the benefit of this is that it can provide a steady stream of income in the form of pension or social security benefits.

Example: An individual starts contributing to their 401(k) at age 25 and retires at age 65. By the time they retire, their 401(k) balance is worth $500,000 and provides a steady stream of income in the form of pension or social security benefits.

Invest in real estate

Another way to create multiple streams of income is to invest in real estate. This can include buying rental properties, becoming a landlord, or flipping houses. The benefit of this is that real estate can provide a steady stream of passive income in the form of rent. Additionally, real estate can also appreciate in value over time, providing the potential for capital gains.

Example: An individual decides to invest in a rental property. They purchase a property for $200,000 and rent it out for $1,500 per month. This provides a steady stream of passive income in the form of rent and the potential for capital gains as the property appreciates in value over time.

Crowdfunding

Crowdfunding is a way to raise money from a large number of people, typically through the internet. Crowdfunding can be used to raise money for a wide range of causes and projects, such as starting a business, creating a product, or producing a film or music album. The benefit of this is that it allows entrepreneurs and creators to raise money quickly and easily without the need for traditional funding sources.

Example: An individual wants to start a business, but they don't have the money. Instead, they use crowdfunding to raise money from a large number of people. They successfully raise $10,000, which they use to start their business.

In conclusion, creating multiple streams of income is a key strategy for achieving financial stability and reaching your financial goals. By having multiple streams of income, you can reduce your dependence on a single source of income, which can help to mitigate financial risks and provide a cushion against unexpected events such as job loss or a downturn in the economy. Remember to consult a financial advisor to help you determine the best strategy for creating multiple streams of income and to ensure that it aligns with your overall financial plan.

How to turn your hobbies and passions into income

Turning your hobbies and passions into income is a great way to monetize your interests and skills while also doing something you love. Here are some ways to turn your hobbies and passions into income and the benefits of doing so:

Sell your creations

If you have a hobby or passion that involves creating something, such as art, crafts, or music, you can sell your creations to make money. The benefit of this is that it allows you to monetize your hobby and also allows you to share your creations with others.

Example: An individual has a passion for knitting. They create scarves, hats, and other items and sell them on Etsy. They make a profit from their sales and also get to share their creations with others.

Offer classes or workshops

If you have a hobby or passion that you are skilled in, you can offer classes or workshops to teach others. The benefit of this is that it allows you to monetize your skills and also allows you to share your knowledge and expertise with others.

Example: An individual has a passion for photography. They offer photography classes and workshops to teach others the basics of photography and make money from the classes.

Start a blog or website

Starting a blog or website on a topic related to your hobby or passion can provide multiple streams of income through advertising, sponsored content, and affiliate marketing. The benefit of this is that it allows you to share your knowledge and expertise with others and also provides an opportunity to monetize your content and audience.

Example: An individual has a passion for gardening. They start a blog about gardening and earn money through advertising, sponsored content, and affiliate marketing. They also have the opportunity to monetize their audience by selling e-books, courses, or consulting services.

Be a consultant

If you have a hobby or passion that involves a specific skill or knowledge, you can offer your expertise as a consultant. The benefit of this is that it allows you to monetize your skills and also allows you to help others.

Example: An individual has a passion for fitness. They become a personal trainer and offer their expertise as a consultant to help others achieve their fitness goals.

Create and sell products

If you have a hobby or passion that involves creating something, such as art, crafts, or music, you can create and sell products related to that hobby or passion. The benefit of this is that it allows you to monetize your hobby and also allows you to share your creations with others.

Example: An individual has a passion for cooking. They create a line of sauces, dressings, and seasoning blends and sell them at local farmer's markets and online. They make a profit from their sales and also get to share their creations with others.

Use Social Media to Promote Your Business

Social media platforms like Facebook, Instagram, and Twitter are powerful tools that can help you promote your business and reach a wider audience. For example, you can use Instagram to showcase your photography skills and attract clients, or use Twitter to share your writing and connect with potential publishers. By building a strong social media presence, you can increase your visibility and credibility, which can lead to more opportunities and more income.

Network and Collaborate with Others

Networking and collaborating with other people in your industry can help you generate new business and income opportunities. For example, if you're a freelance writer, you can reach out to other writers and form a writing group, which can lead to more assignments and better pay. If you're a photographer, you can collaborate with other photographers and create a collective that can offer a wider range of services to clients. By building relationships and working with others, you can increase your income potential and grow your business.

Create a membership or subscription service

Another way to turn your hobby into income is to create a membership or subscription service. For example, if you enjoy cooking, you can create a meal plan subscription service that sends customers a new recipe every week. If you enjoy photography, you can create a monthly photo challenge subscription service where members receive a different photography challenge each month. This model can provide a steady stream of income and can be a great way to engage with your customers and build a loyal following.

In conclusion, turning your hobbies and passions into income is a great way to monetize your interests and skills while also doing something you love. Remember to focus on your strengths.

How to start your own business

Starting your own business can be a challenging but rewarding endeavor. It requires a lot of hard work, dedication, and planning, but the rewards can be great. Whether you're starting a small online business or a brick-and-mortar store, there are many things to consider when starting your own business. In this chapter, we will explore some of the steps you need to take to start your own business, with detailed examples and explanations.

Identify your business idea

The first step in starting your own business is to identify your business idea. This means deciding what product or service you want to offer, and to whom. For example, if you're interested in fashion, you might want to start an online clothing store that specializes in sustainable, ethically-made clothing. If you're interested in fitness, you might want to start a personal training business that helps people achieve their fitness goals. It's important to choose a business idea that you're passionate about and that you believe in, as this will help you stay motivated and focused.

Conduct market research

Once you have identified your business idea, the next step is to conduct market research. This means researching your target market, your competitors, and the overall industry. For example, if you're starting an online clothing store, you'll want to research the fashion industry, the latest trends, and what other online clothing stores are already out there. By conducting market research, you can gain a better understanding of your target market and how your business fits into the industry.

Create a business plan

A business plan is a document that outlines your business idea, target market, marketing strategy, financial projections, and other important information. It's a crucial step in starting your own business, as it helps you to organize your thoughts and identify potential challenges. For example, if you're starting an online clothing store, your business plan might include details about your target market, your suppliers, your marketing strategy, and your financial projections. By creating a business plan, you can gain a better understanding of your business and how it will operate.

Secure funding

Once you have a business plan, the next step is to secure funding. This can come from a variety of sources, including personal savings, loans, and investments. For example, if you're starting an online clothing store, you might need to secure funding to purchase inventory, build a website, and pay for marketing. It's important to have a clear understanding of how much money you need to start your business and where you will get it.

Register your business and obtain licenses and permits

Before you can start your business, you'll need to register it with your state or local government and obtain any necessary licenses or permits. For example, if you're starting an online clothing store, you'll need to register your business and obtain a sales tax permit. If you're starting a personal training business, you'll need to obtain a business license and any certifications required by your state. By obtaining the necessary licenses and permits, you can ensure that your business is legal and compliant.

Build your team

Starting a business can be a lot of work, and it's important to have a team of people who can help you. For example, if you're starting an online clothing store, you might need to hire a web developer to build your website, a graphic designer to create your branding, and a social media manager to promote your business. By building a team of people who can help you, you can ensure that your business is successful.

In conclusion, starting your own business can be a challenging but rewarding endeavor. It requires careful planning, market research, and a clear understanding of your target market and industry. By identifying your business idea, creating a business plan, securing funding, registering your business, obtaining licenses and permits, building your team, developing an online presence, establishing a pricing strategy, taking care of legal and accounting matters, and launching and promoting your business, you can set your business up for success. Remember that starting a business is a process, and it takes time, effort, and patience to make it successful. Stay focused on your goals, be persistent, and always be open to learning and making adjustments as you go along. With the right mindset and approach, you can turn your business idea into a thriving and profitable enterprise.

How to invest in real estate

Real estate investment can be a great way to build wealth and generate passive income. It can also be a great hedge against inflation and a way to diversify your investment portfolio. However, it's important to understand the various types of real estate investments and the risks and rewards associated with each one. In this chapter, we will explore some of the ways you can invest in real estate, with detailed examples and solutions.

Residential rental properties

One of the most common ways to invest in real estate is by buying and renting out residential properties. This can include single-family homes, duplexes, triplexes, or larger apartment buildings. The goal is to generate rental income and potentially see appreciation in the value of the property over time. For example, if you purchase a single-family home for $200,000 and rent it out for $1,500 per month, you can potentially earn $18,000 per year in rental income. Additionally, if the value of the property appreciates by 3% per year, the property will be worth $234,600 after 10 years.

Commercial properties

Another way to invest in real estate is by buying and renting out commercial properties. This can include office buildings, retail spaces, warehouses, and other types of commercial real estate. The goal is to generate rental income from tenants, such as businesses or corporations. For example, if you purchase a commercial office building for $2,000,000 and rent it out to different businesses for $20 per square foot, you can potentially earn $400,000 per year in rental income.

Fix and flip

Another way to invest in real estate is through fix and flip, which involves buying a property, renovating it, and reselling it for a profit. This can be a great way to generate a quick return on investment, but it also comes with a higher level of risk. For example, if you purchase a fixer-upper property for $150,000, spend $50,000 on renovations, and sell it for $250,000, you can potentially earn a $50,000 profit. However, it's important to note that the real estate market can be unpredictable and there is always a risk that the property may not sell for as much as you had hoped.

Real estate crowdfunding

Another way to invest in real estate is through real estate crowdfunding, which allows investors to pool their money to invest in real estate projects. This can include everything from residential rental properties to commercial properties to fix and flip projects. The goal is to earn a return on investment through rental income, appreciation, or flipping profits. For example, if you invest $5,000 in a real estate crowdfunding platform, and the platform earns a 10% return on investment, you can potentially earn $500 in profits.

REITs (Real Estate Investment Trusts)

A Real Estate Investment Trust (REIT) is a type of security that invests in real estate. REITs allow you to invest in a diversified portfolio of properties, without the need to buy or manage a property yourself. For example, if you invest $10,000 in a REIT, and the REIT earns a 6% return on investment, you can potentially earn $600 in profits.

Investing in real estate can be a great way to build wealth and generate passive income. However, it's important to understand the different types of real estate investments, the risks and rewards associated with each one, and to do your own research before making any investment decisions.

How to Create a Financial Plan and Stick to It

Understanding the importance of a financial plan

Understanding the importance of a financial plan is crucial for achieving financial stability and security. A financial plan is a comprehensive document that outlines an individual's current financial situation, goals, and strategies for achieving those goals. It serves as a roadmap for managing money and making informed financial decisions.

There are several key elements that make up a financial plan. The first is an assessment of an individual's current financial situation. This includes information on income, expenses, assets, liabilities, and net worth. This information is used to determine an individual's overall financial health and identify areas where changes can be made to improve it.

The second element of a financial plan is goal setting. This includes identifying both short-term and long-term financial goals, such as saving for a down payment on a house, paying off credit card debt, or saving for retirement. It's important to set realistic and achievable goals, and to track progress towards them.

The third element of a financial plan is creating a strategy for achieving those goals. This includes developing a budget, creating a savings plan, and identifying investment opportunities. A budget is a plan for allocating money to different expenses, such as housing, food, transportation, and entertainment. A savings plan is a strategy for setting aside money for short-term and long-term goals. Investment opportunities can include stocks, bonds, mutual funds, and real estate.

Finally, a financial plan must be regularly reviewed and updated. This includes monitoring progress towards goals, making adjustments as necessary, and incorporating new information as it becomes available.

Examples of how a financial plan can benefit individuals include:

-A young couple who want to buy their first home, a financial plan can help them identify how much they need to save for a down payment, and how much they can afford to spend on a monthly mortgage payment. -A person who wants to pay off their credit card debt, a financial plan can help them create a budget that allocates enough money to make the minimum payments on all their credit cards, and set a goal to pay off the card with the highest interest rate first. -A person nearing retirement, a financial plan can help them project how much money they'll need to have saved to live comfortably during retirement and identify investment opportunities that can help them achieve that goal.

Overall, a financial plan is an essential tool for managing money and achieving financial goals. It provides a clear picture of an individual's current financial situation, helps set realistic and achievable goals, and provides a roadmap for achieving those goals. Regularly reviewing and updating a financial plan is key to ensuring that it remains relevant and effective in helping individuals achieve financial stability and security.

In addition to the elements already mentioned, a financial plan can also include risk management strategies. This includes insurance coverage for things like health, life, property, and liability. It is important to have the right insurance coverage to protect against unexpected events, such as a medical emergency or a natural disaster. This can help prevent a financial crisis and ensure that an individual has the resources they need to recover.

Another important aspect of a financial plan is estate planning. This includes creating a will or trust, naming beneficiaries, and making arrangements for the distribution of assets upon death. Estate planning can ensure that an individual's assets are distributed according to their wishes and that their loved ones are provided for after they pass away.

An important part of a financial plan is also to consider taxes. This includes understanding how taxes impact different types of income, investments and deductions. It's important to take advantage of tax-saving opportunities, such as 401(k) contributions and charitable donations, to help reduce your tax bill.

A financial plan can also include education planning for children. This includes saving for college tuition and other education expenses, as well as researching financial aid options, scholarships and grants.

For individuals with a business, a financial plan should also include a business plan. This includes setting financial goals for the business, creating a budget, and identifying potential sources of financing. A business plan can also help identify potential risks and opportunities for growth.

Finally, it is important to work with a financial advisor or planner to create and implement a financial plan. They can provide valuable guidance, advice and support to help individuals achieve their financial goals. They also can provide unbiased and objective perspective, and they have access to a wide range of financial products and services that can help to improve an individual's financial situation.

In conclusion, a financial plan is a comprehensive document that outlines an individual's current financial situation, goals and strategies for achieving those goals. It serves as a roadmap for managing money and making informed financial decisions. It includes several key elements such as assessment of the current financial situation, goal setting, creating a strategy, regularly reviewing and updating, and risk management strategies. A financial plan can help individuals achieve financial stability and security, and it is important to work with a financial advisor or planner to create and implement a financial plan.

How to set financial goals

Setting financial goals is an important step towards achieving financial stability and security. A goal is a desired outcome that an individual wants to achieve, and it is important to set specific, measurable and achievable goals that align with an individual's values and priorities.

The first step in setting financial goals is to assess an individual's current financial situation. This includes information on income, expenses, assets, liabilities, and net worth. This information is used to determine an individual's overall financial health and identify areas where changes can be made to improve it.

The next step is to identify both short-term and long-term financial goals. Short-term goals are typically those that can be achieved within a year, while long-term goals are those that will take several years to achieve. It is important to set realistic and achievable goals, and to track progress towards them.

Short-term financial goals examples:

- Building an emergency fund of 3-6 months of expenses.
- Paying off credit card debt
- Saving for a down payment on a car
- Saving for a vacation

Long-term financial goals examples:

- Saving for a down payment on a house
- Paying off student loans
- Saving for retirement
- Saving for children's education

It is important to prioritize the goals and rank them according to importance and urgency. This will help an individual to focus on the most important goals first, and to make sure that they do not spread themselves too thin by trying to achieve too many goals at once.

Once the financial goals are set, the next step is to create a strategy for achieving them. This includes developing a budget, creating a savings plan, and identifying investment opportunities. A budget is a plan for allocating money to different expenses, such as housing, food, transportation, and entertainment. A savings plan is a strategy for setting aside money for short-term and long-term goals. Investment opportunities can include stocks, bonds, mutual funds, and real estate.

To achieve long-term financial goals, it is important to invest money wisely. This includes researching different investment options, understanding the risks and rewards associated with each option, and diversifying investments to spread risk. A financial advisor can help an individual to create a diversified investment portfolio that aligns with their goals, risk tolerance, and time horizon.

It is important to regularly review and update the financial goals. This includes monitoring progress towards goals, making adjustments as necessary, and incorporating new information as it becomes available. If a goal is not met, it is important to reassess the plan and make adjustments to ensure that the goal can be achieved in the future.

Another important aspect of setting financial goals is to break them down into smaller, manageable steps. This can make it easier to achieve the goals and can help to keep an individual motivated. For example, if an individual's goal is to save $10,000 for a down payment on a house, they can break that goal down into smaller goals such as saving $500 per month or $250 per paycheck. This can help to make the goal feel more achievable and can help an individual to track their progress.

It's also crucial to have a timeline for achieving the goals. This can provide a sense of urgency, and it can help an individual to stay focused and on track. For example, if an individual's goal is to pay off credit card debt, they can set a deadline of 12 months to pay it off.

Another way to set financial goals is to set SMART goals. SMART goals are Specific, Measurable, Achievable, Relevant, and Time-bound. Specific goals are clear and defined, measurable goals can be quantified, achievable goals are realistic and attainable, relevant goals align with an individual's values and priorities, and time-bound goals have a deadline. By setting SMART goals, an individual can increase the chances of achieving their goals.

It's also important to have an accountability system in place. This can include regularly checking in with a financial advisor or a trusted friend or family member, setting up automatic savings or investment transfers, or using financial tracking and budgeting tools. Having an accountability system in place can help to keep an individual on track and motivated.

In addition, it's essential to have a plan B. This means that it's important to have a backup plan in case things don't go as planned. For example, if an individual's goal is to save money for a down payment on a house, and they lose their job, they should have a plan in place to minimize expenses or find alternative sources of income.

Finally, it's important to remember that setting financial goals is a continuous process. As an individual's circumstances change, their goals and strategies may need to change as well. It's important to be flexible and open to change, and to be willing to adjust plans as needed.

In conclusion, setting financial goals is an important step towards achieving financial stability and security. It's essential to break them down into smaller, manageable steps, have a timeline, set SMART goals, have an accountability system in place, have a plan B and remember that setting financial goals is a continuous process. Regularly reviewing and updating the financial goals and making adjustments as necessary is crucial for achieving the goals.

How to create a financial plan

Creating a financial plan is an important step towards achieving financial stability and security. A financial plan is a comprehensive document that outlines an individual's current financial situation, goals, and strategies for achieving those goals. It serves as a roadmap for managing money and making informed financial decisions.

There are several key elements that make up a financial plan. The first element is to assess an individual's current financial situation. This includes information on income, expenses, assets, liabilities, and net worth. This information is used to determine an individual's overall financial health and identify areas where changes can be made to improve it.

An individual can gather the necessary information by creating a list of all income sources, including salary, bonuses, rental income, and any other sources of income. The individual should also create a list of all expenses, including housing, food, transportation, entertainment, and any other regular expenses. This will give the individual an idea of how much money they have coming in and going out each month, and will help them identify areas where they may be overspending.

The next step is to identify both short-term and long-term financial goals. Short-term goals are typically those that can be achieved within a year, while long-term goals are those that will take several years to achieve. It's important to set realistic and achievable goals, and to track progress towards them.

Short-term financial goals examples:

- Building an emergency fund of 3-6 months of expenses.

- Paying off credit card debt
- Saving for a down payment on a car
- Saving for a vacation

Long-term financial goals examples:

- Saving for a down payment on a house
- Paying off student loans
- Saving for retirement
- Saving for children's education

The third element of a financial plan is creating a strategy for achieving those goals. This includes developing a budget, creating a savings plan, and identifying investment opportunities. A budget is a plan for allocating money to different expenses, such as housing, food, transportation, and entertainment. A savings plan is a strategy for setting aside money for short-term and long-term goals. Investment opportunities can include stocks, bonds, mutual funds, and real estate.

An individual can create a budget by listing all of their income and expenses, and then allocating money to different expenses. The individual should also set aside money for saving and investing, and make sure that the budget is realistic and achievable.

An individual can create a savings plan by setting up automatic savings transfers or deposit money into a savings account. Investing can be done by researching different investment options, understanding the risks and rewards associated with each option, and diversifying investments to spread risk. A financial advisor can help an individual to create a diversified investment portfolio that aligns with their goals, risk tolerance, and time horizon.

Finally, a financial plan must be regularly reviewed and updated. This includes monitoring progress towards goals, making adjustments as necessary, and incorporating new information as it becomes available.

An example of how a financial plan can benefit an individual is a young couple who wants to buy their first home. A financial plan can help them identify how much they need to save for a down payment, how much they can afford to spend on a monthly mortgage payment, and where they can cut expenses to free up more money for saving and investing.

In conclusion, a financial plan is an essential tool for managing money and achieving financial goals. It provides a clear picture of an individual's current financial situation, helps set realistic and achievable goals, and provides a roadmap for achieving those goals. Creating a financial plan includes assessing an individual's current financial situation, identifying both short-term and long-term financial goals, creating a strategy for achieving those goals, and regularly reviewing and updating the plan. The process includes gathering information on income, expenses, assets, liabilities, and net worth, creating a budget and savings plan, and identifying investment opportunities. It's important to prioritize and rank the goals according to importance and urgency, and to work with a financial advisor or planner if necessary.

It is also important to be flexible and open to change, and to be willing to adjust the plan as needed. A financial plan should be a living document that adapts to an individual's changing circumstances, and it is essential to regularly review and update the plan to ensure that it remains relevant and effective in helping individuals achieve financial stability and security.

In addition, it is crucial to have a clear understanding of the key concepts and principles of personal finance, such as budgeting, saving, and investing, in order to create an effective financial plan.

Overall, creating a financial plan is an important step towards achieving financial stability and security. It provides a clear picture of an individual's current financial situation, helps set realistic and achievable goals, and provides a roadmap for achieving those goals. With a detailed financial plan in place, individuals can make informed decisions, manage their money effectively, and work towards achieving their financial goals.

Tips for sticking to your financial plan

Sticking to a financial plan is crucial for achieving financial stability and security. A financial plan is a comprehensive document that outlines an individual's current financial situation, goals, and strategies for achieving those goals. However, creating a financial plan is just the first step, the real challenge is sticking to it. Here are some tips for sticking to your financial plan.

Set realistic and achievable goals

It's important to set realistic and achievable goals that align with an individual's values and priorities. Setting goals that are too ambitious can lead to frustration and disappointment, and make it difficult to stick to the plan.

Prioritize and rank your goals

Prioritizing and ranking your goals according to importance and urgency can help you to focus on the most important goals first, and make sure that you don't spread yourself too thin by trying to achieve too many goals at once.

Create a budget and stick to it

Creating a budget and sticking to it is key to sticking to a financial plan. A budget is a plan for allocating money to different expenses, such as housing, food, transportation, and entertainment. It's important to review the budget regularly, and make adjustments as necessary.

Automate your savings

Automating your savings can make it easier to stick to a financial plan. For example, setting up automatic savings transfers or deposit money into a savings account can help to ensure that you are setting aside money for short-term and long-term goals.

Track your progress

Tracking your progress can help you stay motivated and on track. It's important to regularly review your financial plan, and track your progress towards your goals. This can help you to identify areas where you may be falling behind, and make adjustments as necessary.

Be accountable

Having an accountability system in place can help you to stick to your financial plan. This can include regularly checking in with a financial advisor or a trusted friend or family member, setting up automatic savings or investment transfers, or using financial tracking and budgeting tools.

Stay flexible

Life is unpredictable, and it's important to be flexible and open to change. A financial plan should be a living document that adapts to an individual's changing circumstances. It's important to be willing to adjust your plan as needed.

Reward yourself

Reward yourself when you achieve your goals, it can help you stay motivated. For example, if you achieve your saving goal for a vacation, you can plan and book the vacation as a reward.

An example of how these tips can help an individual stick to their financial plan is a young couple who wants to buy their first home. They set a realistic and achievable goal of saving for a 20% down payment on a house within two years. They prioritize and rank their goals by focusing on saving for the down payment as their top priority. They create a budget and stick to it, by cutting unnecessary expenses and setting up automatic savings transfers. They track their progress by reviewing their savings account regularly, and make adjustments as necessary. They hold each other accountable by regularly discussing their progress and sticking to their budget. They stay flexible by adjusting their plan if they encounter unexpected expenses or changes in income. And they reward themselves by celebrating milestones along the way, such as reaching half of their down payment savings goal.

Another example is an individual who wants to pay off credit card debt. The individual sets a realistic and achievable goal to pay off the debt within 12 months. They prioritize and rank their goals by focusing on paying off the credit card debt as their top priority. They create a budget and stick to it, by cutting unnecessary expenses and setting up automatic payments to their credit card.

They track their progress by reviewing their credit card statement regularly, and make adjustments as necessary. They hold themselves accountable by setting reminders to make payments and regularly reviewing their progress. They stay flexible by adjusting their plan if they encounter unexpected expenses or changes in income. And they reward themselves by celebrating milestones along the way, such as paying off half of their credit card debt.

In conclusion, sticking to a financial plan is crucial for achieving financial stability and security. Creating a financial plan is just the first step, the real challenge is sticking to it. Tips for sticking to a financial plan include setting realistic and achievable goals, prioritizing and ranking goals, creating a budget and sticking to it, automating savings, tracking progress, being accountable, staying flexible and rewarding yourself along the way. These tips can help individuals to stay motivated and on track, and to make adjustments as necessary to ensure that they achieve their financial goals.

How to track your progress

Tracking your progress is an important step towards achieving financial stability and security. It allows you to monitor your progress towards your financial goals, identify areas where you may be falling behind, and make adjustments as necessary. Here are some tips for tracking your progress.

Use a budgeting app or spreadsheet

One of the easiest ways to track your progress is to use a budgeting app or spreadsheet. These tools allow you to input your income, expenses, and savings, and track your progress over time. They also allow you to see where your money is going and identify areas where you may be overspending.

Set up automatic savings

Setting up automatic savings transfers or deposit money into a savings account can help to ensure that you are setting aside money for short-term and long-term goals. Many banks and financial institutions offer automatic savings options, and you can track your progress by regularly reviewing your account balance.

Monitor your credit score

Monitoring your credit score is important for tracking your progress towards your financial goals. A good credit score is important for getting approved for loans, credit cards, and mortgages. You can monitor your credit score for free at various websites like Credit Karma, Credit Sesame or use free credit monitoring services from your bank or credit card issuer.

Review your investments

Reviewing your investments is an important part of tracking your progress. This includes monitoring the performance of your investments and making adjustments as necessary. It's important to regularly review your investment portfolio, and to make sure that it is diversified and aligned with your goals, risk tolerance, and time horizon.

Review your progress regularly

Reviewing your progress regularly is essential for tracking your progress towards your financial goals. This includes regularly reviewing your budget, savings, credit score, and investments. It's also important to review your progress towards your financial goals, and to make adjustments as necessary.

An example of how tracking progress can help an individual achieve their financial goals is a young couple who wants to buy their first home. They set a goal of saving for a 20% down payment on a house within two years. They use a budgeting app to track their income, expenses, and savings. They also set up automatic savings transfers to their savings account and monitor their credit score regularly. They also review their investments and re-balance their portfolio as necessary. They review their progress regularly and make adjustments as necessary to ensure that they are on track to achieve their goal.

In conclusion, tracking your progress is an important step towards achieving financial stability and security. It allows you to monitor your progress towards your financial goals, identify areas where you may be falling behind, and make adjustments as necessary. Tips for tracking your progress include using a budgeting app or spreadsheet, setting up automatic savings, monitoring your credit score, reviewing your investments, and reviewing your progress regularly. By regularly monitoring and tracking your progress, you can ensure that you are on track to achieving your financial goals.

Building Wealth Through Real Estate

How to research and choose real estate investments

Researching and choosing real estate investments is an important step in achieving financial stability and security through real estate investing. It's important to do your due diligence and to carefully research potential investments in order to make informed decisions and minimize risks. Here are some tips for researching and choosing real estate investments:

Understand your investment goals

Before researching and choosing real estate investments, it's important to have a clear understanding of your investment goals. This includes understanding your risk tolerance, time horizon, and cash flow needs.

Research the market

Researching the market is an important step in choosing real estate investments. This includes researching the local real estate market, including supply and demand, economic conditions, and demographic trends. It's also important to research the specific property and neighborhood, including the property's condition, age, and location.

Consider the property's cash flow

Cash flow is the amount of money that an investment property generates after all expenses are paid. It's important to consider the property's cash flow, as well as the potential for future cash flow, when choosing real estate investments.

Look for properties with potential for appreciation

Appreciation is the increase in the value of a property over time. It's important to look for properties with potential for appreciation, as this can provide a source of capital gains when the property is sold.

Get a professional opinion

It's important to get a professional opinion, such as a real estate agent or a property inspector, when researching and choosing real estate investments. This can help you to make more informed decisions and to identify potential issues that may not be immediately obvious.

An example of how researching and choosing real estate investments can help an individual achieve their financial goals is a young entrepreneur who wants to diversify their investment portfolio. They understand their investment goals, which is to generate cash flow and capital appreciation for their portfolio diversification. They research different types of real estate investments such as REITs, rental properties, and commercial properties. They also research different markets, such as the local market, where they are familiar with the area and have a good understanding of the local economy and demographics, and also look for opportunities in other markets, such as vacation rental properties in popular tourist destinations. They also consider the property's cash flow, as well as the potential for future cash flow, when choosing real estate investments. They also look for properties with potential for appreciation, and also get professional opinions from real estate agents and property inspectors to help them identify potential issues and make more informed decisions.

In this example, the entrepreneur conducts a thorough research and due diligence, to make sure they are making a well-informed decision, they also diversify their investments across different types of real estate and markets, which helps to spread risk and maximize potential returns.

Another example of how researching and choosing real estate investments can help an individual achieve their financial goals is a retiree who wants to generate passive income for their retirement. They understand their investment goals, which is to generate steady cash flow through rental income. They research different types of rental properties, such as single-family homes, duplexes, and apartment buildings, in the area they are familiar with. They also research the local rental market, including the average rental rates, vacancy rates, and demand for rental properties. They also consider the property's potential cash flow, as well as the potential for future cash flow, when choosing real estate investments. They also get professional opinions from real estate agents and property managers to help them identify potential issues and make more informed decisions.

In this example, the retiree's focus is to generate steady cash flow through rental income which will help to support their lifestyle during retirement, they also focus on the area they are familiar with, so they can have a good understanding of the local rental market and rental properties. By choosing rental properties, the retiree can enjoy a steady stream of passive income, helping them to achieve their financial goals.

In conclusion, researching and choosing real estate investments is an important step in achieving financial stability and security through real estate investing. It's important to do your due diligence and to carefully research potential investments in order to make informed decisions and minimize risks. Tips for researching and choosing real estate investments include understanding your investment goals, researching the market, considering the property's cash flow, looking for properties with potential for appreciation, and getting a professional opinion. By following these guidelines, individuals can make informed decisions and achieve their financial goals through real estate investing.

How to manage and maintain a rental property

Managing and maintaining a rental property is an important aspect of real estate investing. It's important to properly manage and maintain a rental property in order to attract and retain tenants, increase cash flow, and maintain the value of the property. Here are some tips for managing and maintaining a rental property:

Screen tenants

It's important to screen tenants to ensure that they will be responsible and reliable renters. This includes conducting background checks, credit checks, and landlord reference checks.

Set rent at the right price

It's important to set the rent at the right price in order to attract and retain tenants. This includes researching the local rental market, including the average rental rates and vacancy rates, in order to determine the appropriate rent.

Regularly maintain and upgrade the property

Regularly maintaining and upgrading the property can help to attract and retain tenants and also increase the value of the property over time. This includes regular cleaning and repairs, as well as upgrades such as painting, flooring, and appliances.

Respond promptly to tenant complaints and requests

Responding promptly to tenant complaints and requests can help to maintain a positive relationship with tenants and retain them as renters.

Hire a property manager

If you don't have the time or expertise to manage and maintain a rental property, it may be worth hiring a property manager. A property manager can handle the day-to-day tasks of managing and maintaining a rental property, such as finding tenants, collecting rent, and handling repairs and maintenance.

An example of how managing and maintaining a rental property can help an individual achieve their financial goals is a retiree who wants to generate passive income for their retirement. They invest in a rental property and screen tenants carefully to ensure that they are responsible and reliable renters. They set the rent at the right price by researching the local rental market, and regularly maintain and upgrade the property. They also respond promptly to tenant complaints and requests, which helps to maintain a positive relationship with tenants and retain them as renters. By managing and maintaining the rental property effectively, the retiree is able to generate a steady stream of passive income to support their lifestyle during retirement.

Managing and maintaining a rental property is an important aspect of real estate investing. It's important to properly manage and maintain a rental property in order to attract and retain tenants, increase cash flow, and maintain the value of the property. Tips for managing and maintaining a rental property include screening tenants, setting rent at the right price, regularly maintaining and upgrading the property, responding promptly to tenant complaints and requests, and hiring a property manager if needed. By following these guidelines, individuals can achieve their financial goals through real estate investing by generating passive income through rental properties.

Another example of how managing and maintaining a rental property can help an individual achieve their financial goals is a young couple who wants to purchase a duplex as an investment property. They research the local rental market and set the rent at a competitive price to attract tenants. They also make sure to conduct regular maintenance and repairs to keep the property in good condition. They also have a strict policy for late rent payments and eviction process in case of non-payment. They also have a good relationship with their tenants and respond promptly to any complaints or requests. They also budget for unexpected repairs and expenses, such as emergency repairs or major renovation projects. By managing and maintaining the rental property effectively, the young couple is able to generate a steady stream of passive income and also has a valuable asset that appreciates over time.

In conclusion, managing and maintaining a rental property is an important aspect of real estate investing. It's important to properly manage and maintain a rental property to attract and retain tenants, increase cash flow, and maintain the value of the property. Tips for managing and maintaining a rental property include setting rent at the right price, regularly maintaining and upgrading the property, responding promptly to tenant complaints and requests, and having a plan for unexpected expenses. It's also important to have a good relationship with your tenants and to be responsive to their needs. By following these guidelines, individuals can achieve their financial goals through real estate investing by generating passive income through rental properties and also having a valuable asset that appreciates over time.

How to exit a real estate investment

Exiting a real estate investment is an important aspect of real estate investing. It's important to have a plan for exiting a real estate investment in order to maximize returns and minimize losses. There are several ways to exit a real estate investment, including:

Selling the property

Selling the property is one of the most common ways to exit a real estate investment. This can include listing the property for sale on the open market or selling it to a real estate investor or developer.

Refinancing

Refinancing is another way to exit a real estate investment. This can include taking out a new loan on the property to pay off the existing loan and provide cash for other investments.

Renting the property

Renting the property is a way to generate passive income while maintaining ownership of the property. This can include renting the property to tenants on a long-term or short-term basis.

Rent-to-own

Rent-to-own is a way to sell the property while providing tenants with the opportunity to purchase the property over time. This can include renting the property to tenants with the option to purchase the property at a later date.

An example of how exiting a real estate investment can help an individual achieve their financial goals is a young entrepreneur who wants to generate cash for other investments. They purchase a rental property and hold on to it for several years, during which time they generate passive income from rent. They then sell the property for a profit, which they use to invest in other opportunities such as stock market or a new business venture.

Another example of how exiting a real estate investment can help an individual achieve their financial goals is a retiree who wants to generate passive income and maintain ownership of a property. They purchase a vacation rental property and rent it out on a short-term basis. They generate a steady stream of passive income from rent, and when they are ready to exit the investment, they can decide to continue renting it out or list it for sale on the open market.

Exiting a real estate investment is an important aspect of real estate investing. It's important to have a plan for exiting a real estate investment in order to maximize returns and minimize losses. There are several ways to exit a real estate investment, including selling the property, refinancing, renting the property, and rent-to-own. It's important to consider your investment goals and risk tolerance when deciding how to exit a real estate investment. By having a clear exit plan, individuals can achieve their financial goals through real estate investing by generating cash flow and capital appreciation.

Another example of how exiting a real estate investment can help an individual achieve their financial goals is a family who wants to invest in a property with the intention of holding it for the long-term. They purchase a multi-family property and hold on to it for several years, during which time they generate passive income from rent. They also conduct regular maintenance and upgrades to the property to increase its value over time. After several years, they decide to refinance the property and take out a new loan to extract equity from the property for their other investments or for their children's education.

Another example of exiting a real estate investment is a property developer who is looking to generate cash flow and also increase the value of the property. They purchase a property with the intention of renovating and flipping it. They conduct a thorough market research and also get professional opinions, after which they conduct the necessary repairs and upgrades to the property. They then list the property for sale and exit the investment by selling the property at a higher price, generating a profit that they can use to fund their next project.

In conclusion, exiting a real estate investment is an important aspect of real estate investing. It's important to have a plan for exiting a real estate investment in order to maximize returns and minimize losses. There are several ways to exit a real estate investment, including selling the property, refinancing, renting the property, and rent-to-own. It's important to consider your investment goals and risk tolerance when deciding how to exit a real estate investment. By having a clear exit plan, individuals can achieve their financial goals through real estate investing by generating cash flow and capital appreciation, and also by extracting equity from the property.

The Power of Networking and Building Business Relationships

Understanding the importance of networking

Networking is one of the most powerful tools you have at your disposal when it comes to building wealth. It is the process of building relationships with other people in order to achieve your goals. In this chapter, we will explore the importance of networking and provide some examples of how it can help you achieve financial success.

One of the most important benefits of networking is that it allows you to access opportunities that you may not have been aware of otherwise. For example, if you are a job seeker looking for a new opportunity, networking can help you learn about job openings before they are publicly advertised. This can give you a significant advantage over other applicants.

Networking can also help you build relationships with people who can help you advance your career. For example, if you are an entrepreneur, networking can help you connect with potential investors or partners who can help you grow your business.

Another important benefit of networking is that it allows you to gain insights and advice from people who have more experience than you. For example, if you are a new investor, networking with more experienced investors can help you learn about different investment strategies and avoid mistakes that they may have made in the past.

Networking can also help you build a support system of people who can help you through difficult times. For example, if you are facing financial challenges, networking with people who have been through similar experiences can help you find solutions and get the support you need to overcome them.

Networking can help you build a sense of community and belonging. For example, if you are a business owner, networking with other business owners can help you feel less alone and more connected to others who understand the challenges you are facing.

In order to effectively network and build relationships that can help you achieve your financial goals, it's important to understand a few key principles.

First, it's important to be intentional about building your network. Don't just wait for opportunities to come to you - actively seek out people and organizations that can help you achieve your goals. This might mean attending networking events, joining professional organizations, or even reaching out to people you admire on social media.

Next, it's important to build genuine relationships, not just collect contacts. This means taking the time to get to know people and understand their goals and needs, as well as being willing to share your own goals and needs.

Another important principle is to be generous. Networking is not just about what you can get out of it, but also about what you can give. This might mean offering to help people in your network achieve their goals, or offering to connect them with people in your own network.

Finally, it's important to be consistent in your networking efforts. Building a strong network takes time and effort, so it's important to make networking a regular part of your routine. This might mean setting aside time each week to attend networking events or reach out to people in your network.

To give you an example, let's say you're a recent college graduate looking for a job in the finance industry. You could start by attending job fairs and networking events hosted by finance companies, reaching out to alumni in the finance industry and asking if they would be willing to meet with you and share their experiences, and joining professional organizations like the Financial Executives Networking Group (FENG) or the National Association of Black Accountants (NABA). By being intentional, building genuine relationships, being generous, and being consistent, you'll be able to grow your network and increase your chances of finding the right job in the finance industry.

In summary, networking is a vital tool for building wealth. It allows you to access opportunities, gain insights and advice, build a support system, and create a sense of community. To be effective at networking, it's important to be intentional, build genuine relationships, be generous, and be consistent. Start building your network today and you will be well on your way to achieving your financial goals.

How to build a strong network

Building a strong network is essential for achieving financial success, whether you're a job seeker looking for a new opportunity, an entrepreneur looking for investors or partners, or an established professional looking to advance your career. In this chapter, we will explore the key principles of networking and provide specific examples of how to build a strong network.

The first principle of networking is to be intentional. Don't wait for opportunities to come to you - actively seek out people and organizations that can help you achieve your goals. This might mean attending networking events, joining professional organizations, or even reaching out to people you admire on social media.

For example, let's say you're an entrepreneur looking for investors for your startup. You could start by attending networking events and conferences specific to your industry, joining online groups and forums for entrepreneurs and startup enthusiasts, and reaching out to venture capitalists and angel investors directly. By being intentional, you increase the chances of connecting with potential investors who can help you grow your business.

The second principle of networking is to build genuine relationships, not just collect contacts. This means taking the time to get to know people and understand their goals and needs, as well as being willing to share your own goals and needs.

For example, let's say you're a job seeker looking for a new opportunity. Instead of just handing out your resume at a networking event, take the time to have a conversation with people you meet. Ask about their experiences, what they're looking for in a candidate, and how you might be able to help them. By building a genuine relationship, you increase the likelihood that they will remember you and think of you when an opportunity arises.

The third principle of networking is to be generous. Networking is not just about what you can get out of it, but also about what you can give. This might mean offering to help people in your network achieve their goals, or offering to connect them with people in your own network.

For example, let's say you're a consultant and you've just completed a project for a client. Instead of just thanking them and moving on, ask if there is anyone in their network that they think might benefit from your services. By being generous, you're not only helping them, but also potentially gaining new clients in the process.

The fourth principle of networking is to be consistent in your efforts. Building a strong network takes time and effort, so it's important to make networking a regular part of your routine. This might mean setting aside time each week to attend networking events or reach out to people in your network.

For example, you could schedule a monthly coffee meeting with a colleague or friend in your network, send a monthly newsletter to your network with updates on your professional life, or even a yearly event to bring together the people you've met during the year. By consistently reaching out to people and staying in touch, you'll keep your network strong and active.

In conclusion, networking is a vital tool for building wealth. By following these key principles and putting them into practice, you can build a strong network that will help you achieve your financial goals. Remember to be intentional, build genuine relationships, be generous, and be consistent. Building a strong network takes time and effort, but the rewards are well worth it.

How to use your network to achieve financial success

One of the most powerful ways to achieve financial success is by leveraging the power of your network. Your network is made up of the people you know and the relationships you have built with them. By using your network effectively, you can access new opportunities, gain valuable insights and advice, and build a support system that can help you navigate the challenges of building wealth. In this chapter, we will explore how to use your network to achieve financial success, with detailed examples.

First, let's consider how your network can help you access new opportunities. For example, if you're a job seeker looking for a new opportunity, your network can help you learn about job openings before they are publicly advertised. This can give you a significant advantage over other applicants.

For example, let's say you're a recent college graduate looking for a job in the finance industry. You could reach out to people in your network who work in finance, and ask if they know of any job openings in their company or other companies they are aware of. By using your network to learn about job openings, you increase your chances of getting hired and achieving your goal of finding a job in the finance industry.

Your network can also help you gain valuable insights and advice from people who have more experience than you. For example, if you're a new investor, your network can help you learn about different investment strategies and avoid mistakes that other investors may have made in the past.

For example, let's say you're a new investor and you want to learn about real estate investing. You could reach out to people in your network who have experience in real estate investing, and ask if they would be willing to share their experiences and advice with you. By gaining insights and advice from experienced investors, you can make better-informed investment decisions and increase your chances of achieving financial success.

Your network can also help you build a support system of people who can help you through difficult times. For example, if you're facing financial challenges, your network can help you find solutions and get the support you need to overcome them.

For example, let's say you're a small business owner and your business is struggling. You could reach out to people in your network who have experience running a business and ask for their advice and support. They may be able to provide you with valuable insights and help you navigate the challenges you're facing.

Finally, your network can help you build a sense of community and belonging. For example, if you're a business owner, your network can help you feel less alone and more connected to others who understand the challenges you're facing.

For example, you could join a local business association or a Meetup group where other business owners in your area come together to share their experiences and support each other. By being part of a community of like-minded individuals, you can feel more connected and supported, which can help you achieve your financial goals.

In conclusion, your network is a powerful tool that can help you achieve financial success. By using your network to access new opportunities, gain valuable insights and advice, build a support system, and create a sense of community, you can increase your chances of achieving your financial goals. Remember to be intentional, build genuine relationships, be generous, and be consistent in your networking efforts. By doing so, you will be able to leverage the power of your network and achieve financial success.

How to build long-term business relationships

Building long-term business relationships is essential for achieving success in any industry. Strong relationships with clients, partners, vendors, and other industry professionals can help you secure new business, increase sales, and gain access to valuable resources and information. In this chapter, we will explore the key principles of building long-term business relationships, and provide detailed examples of how to put these principles into practice.

The first principle of building long-term business relationships is to be reliable and dependable. This means being consistent in your communication, meeting deadlines, and delivering high-quality products or services. When people know they can rely on you, they are more likely to do business with you in the long-term.

For example, let's say you're a freelance graphic designer and you've been working with a client for a few months. You've consistently met deadlines, delivered high-quality designs, and been responsive to their requests for revisions. The client is happy with the work you've done and will be more likely to continue working with you in the future.

The second principle of building long-term business relationships is to be transparent and honest. This means being upfront about your strengths and weaknesses, and being willing to admit when you make a mistake. When people trust you, they are more likely to do business with you in the long-term.

For example, let's say you're a vendor for a company and you've been working with them for a few years. One day you realize that you've made a mistake and you're going to be late delivering a product. You immediately contact the client and explain the situation, apologize and give them an estimated time of delivery. They understand and appreciate your honesty and transparency, and are more likely to continue working with you in the future.

The third principle of building long-term business relationships is to be proactive. This means going above and beyond what is expected, and offering solutions or suggestions for how to improve products or services. When people see that you're committed to helping them succeed, they are more likely to do business with you in the long-term.

For example, let's say you're an account manager for a company and you've been working with a client for a few years. You notice that they're having trouble generating leads and closing deals. You suggest they try a new marketing strategy and offer to help them implement it. The client is impressed by your proactive approach and is more likely to continue working with you in the future.

The fourth principle of building long-term business relationships is to be responsive. This means being available to answer questions, address concerns, and provide support in a timely manner. When people know they can reach out to you and get a quick response, they are more likely to do business with you in the long-term.

For example, let's say you're a consultant for a company and you've been working with a client for a few months. They've reached out to you with some questions about the project and you respond promptly. The client is impressed by your responsiveness and is more likely to continue working with you in the future.

In conclusion, building long-term business relationships is essential for achieving success in any industry. By being reliable, transparent, proactive, and responsive, you can create strong relationships with clients, partners, vendors, and other industry professionals that will help you secure new business, increase sales, and gain access to valuable resources and information. Remember that building long-term business relationships takes time, effort and consistent actions, but the rewards are well worth it.

CHAPTER TEN

How to Retire Early and Achieve Financial Independence

Understanding the concept of financial independence

Financial independence is the state of having enough wealth to support oneself without having to rely on traditional sources of income, such as a job or government benefits. It is the ability to live the life you want, free from the constraints of financial worry. In this chapter, we will explore the concept of financial independence and provide detailed examples of how to achieve it.

The first step in achieving financial independence is to understand your current financial situation. This includes understanding your income, expenses, assets, and liabilities. By understanding your current financial situation, you can identify areas where you can cut expenses and increase income, which will help you save more money.

For example, let's say you're earning $60,000 a year and your expenses are $50,000 a year. This means you're saving $10,000 a year. However, upon analyzing your expenses you realize that you're spending $3000 a year on subscription services you don't use and eating out more than you should, cutting those expenses would give you an additional $5000 a year to save.

The second step is to create a savings plan. This includes setting financial goals, such as saving for retirement or a down payment on a house, and creating a budget to ensure that you're saving enough money to reach those goals. A budget can help you see where your money is going and make adjustments to your spending, so you can save more.

For example, let's say you want to save $50,000 for a down payment on a house in the next five years. To reach this goal, you need to save $10,000 a year, or $833 a month. By creating a budget and cutting unnecessary expenses, you can ensure that you're saving enough money to reach your goal.

The third step is to invest your money wisely. This includes understanding the different types of investments, such as stocks, bonds, and real estate, and choosing investments that align with your financial goals and risk tolerance. Investing your money will help it grow and compound over time, which will help you achieve financial independence.

For example, let's say you're saving $10,000 a year and you want to retire in 30 years. If you invest that money in a portfolio that returns an average of 7% a year, in 30 years, you'll have over $1 million dollars. This will give you the flexibility to retire or have options to not rely on a traditional job to support yourself.

The fourth step is to live below your means. This means spending less than you earn, and avoiding lifestyle inflation, which is the tendency to increase spending as income increases. By living below your means, you can save more money and invest more money, which will help you achieve financial independence faster.

For example, let's say you get a raise and your income increases from $60,000 a year to $70,000 a year. Instead of increasing your spending, you continue to live on $60,000 a year and save the additional $10,000 a year. By living below your means, you're able to save more money and reach financial independence faster.

In conclusion, financial independence is the ability to support oneself without having to rely on traditional sources of income. It can be achieved by understanding your current financial situation, creating a savings plan, investing your money wisely, and living below your means. By following these steps and making smart financial decisions, you can achieve financial independence and live the life you want, free from financial worry.

How to calculate your number

Your "number" refers to the amount of money you need to have saved and invested in order to achieve financial independence and retire. It is a crucial concept to understand when planning for retirement, as it helps you determine how much you need to save and invest in order to reach your financial goals. In this chapter, we will explore how to calculate your number and provide detailed examples of how to put this concept into practice.

The first step in calculating your number is to determine your annual expenses. This includes all of your fixed expenses, such as housing, transportation, and food, as well as any variable expenses, such as entertainment and travel. Add all of these expenses together to get your total annual expenses.

For example, let's say your fixed expenses are $40,000 a year, and your variable expenses are $20,000 a year. Your total annual expenses would be $60,000 a year.

The second step is to determine your annual income from other sources, such as pensions, Social Security, or rental income. Add this to your total annual expenses to determine your total annual income need.

For example, let's say you're expecting to receive $20,000 a year from Social Security and $10,000 a year from rental income. Your total annual income need is $90,000 a year.

The third step is to determine your withdrawal rate, which is the percentage of your savings you can safely withdraw each year without running out of money. A common withdrawal rate is 4%. Multiply your total annual income need by 25 (1 / 0.04) to determine your total savings needed to achieve financial independence.

For example, $90,000 x 25 = $2,250,000. This means you would need to have $2,250,000 saved and invested in order to achieve financial independence and retire, assuming a 4% withdrawal rate.

The fourth step is to adjust your number for any additional income or savings you expect to have in retirement. This could include rental income from properties you own, income from a part-time job, or other sources of income.

For example, let's say you own a rental property and expect to receive $15,000 a year in rental income. You would subtract that from your total annual income need and the number would be $75,000 a year. Then you would calculate your number again, $75,000 x 25 = $1,875,000, this would be your new number with that additional income source.

It's also important to keep in mind that these numbers are estimates and that there are many factors that can affect your number and your ability to achieve financial independence. Inflation, unexpected expenses, and changes in investment returns can all affect your number and the timeline for achieving financial independence. It's important to regularly review and update your number as your expenses, income, and goals change over time.

Another important factor to consider is the lifestyle you want to have in retirement. If you have plans to travel extensively, have a bigger house or a second home, or have other expensive hobbies, you will need to factor those expenses in your calculation and adjust your number accordingly.

It's also important to remember that achieving financial independence is not a one-time event, but rather a continuous process of saving, investing, and planning for the future. It's important to have a plan in place and to make consistent efforts to save and invest for your future.

In conclusion, calculating your number is an important step in achieving financial independence and retirement. It involves determining your annual expenses, income needs, and withdrawal rate, and adjusting for additional income and lifestyle choices. Remember that your number is an estimate and that it may change over time. It's important to regularly review and update your number as your expenses, income, and goals change, and to make consistent efforts to save and invest for your future.

How to invest for retirement

Investing for retirement is a crucial step in achieving financial independence and securing a comfortable future. By investing your money wisely, you can grow your savings and build wealth over time. In this chapter, we will explore how to invest for retirement and provide detailed examples of how to put this concept into practice.

The first step in investing for retirement is to determine your investment goals and risk tolerance. Your investment goals should align with your overall financial goals, such as saving for a down payment on a house or achieving financial independence. Your risk tolerance refers to your willingness to take on risk in exchange for potential returns. Understanding your investment goals and risk tolerance will help you choose the right investment vehicles for your portfolio.

For example, let's say your goal is to save for retirement in 25 years, you will have a long-term horizon and therefore you can afford to take on a higher level of risk and invest in equities.

The second step is to diversify your portfolio. Diversification means spreading your money across different types of investments, such as stocks, bonds, and real estate. This helps to reduce risk and increase potential returns. A well-diversified portfolio will typically include a mix of stocks, bonds, and real estate.

For example, you could invest 60% of your money in stocks, 30% in bonds, and 10% in real estate. This diversification strategy helps to spread the risk across different types of investments, reducing the impact of any one investment on your overall portfolio.

The third step is to choose the right investment vehicles. Investment vehicles are the specific products, such as mutual funds or exchange-traded funds (ETFs), that you use to invest your money. It's important to choose investment vehicles that align with your investment goals and risk tolerance.

For example, if you're a conservative investor, you may choose to invest in bond funds or target-date retirement funds. These types of funds tend to be less risky and provide more stable returns. On the other hand, if you're a more aggressive investor, you may choose to invest in stock funds or real estate investment trusts (REITs). These types of funds tend to be more risky but offer the potential for higher returns.

The fourth step is to regularly review and rebalance your portfolio. This means reviewing your portfolio on a regular basis, such as annually, and making adjustments as needed. This can include buying or selling investments, or adjusting the mix of investments in your portfolio. It's important to regularly review your portfolio to ensure that it aligns with your investment goals and risk tolerance and that your investments are performing as expected.

For example, let's say you have a portfolio that is 60% stocks, 30% bonds, and 10% real estate. After a year, the value of your stocks has grown by 20%, while the value of your bonds has only grown by 5%. This means that your portfolio is now more heavily weighted towards stocks, which may not align with your risk tolerance. To rebalance, you could sell some of your stock investments and buy more bond investments to bring your portfolio back to its original 60/30/10 allocation.

In conclusion, investing for retirement is a crucial step in achieving financial independence and securing a comfortable future. It involves determining your investment goals and risk tolerance, diversifying your portfolio, choosing the right investment vehicles, and regularly reviewing and rebalancing your portfolio. By following these steps and making smart investment decisions, you can grow your savings and build wealth over time, positioning yourself for a successful retirement.

CHAPTER ELEVEN

Legacy Planning and Building Wealth for Future Generations

Understanding the importance of legacy planning

Legacy planning is the process of creating a plan to ensure that your assets and values are passed on to future generations in a way that aligns with your goals and values. It goes beyond just financial planning and includes creating a plan for your personal and family values, beliefs, and traditions. In this chapter, we will explore the importance of legacy planning and provide detailed examples of how to put this concept into practice.

The first step in legacy planning is to understand your values and goals. This includes understanding your family's history, culture, and traditions, as well as your personal values and beliefs. By understanding your values and goals, you can create a plan that aligns with them and ensure that they are passed on to future generations.

For example, let's say your family has a tradition of supporting education, you could consider setting up a scholarship fund in your family's name to ensure that this tradition continues for generations to come.

The second step is to create a plan for your assets. This includes creating a will, trust, or other legal documents that outline how your assets will be distributed after your death. It also includes ensuring that your assets are properly titled and that there are clear instructions for their distribution.

For example, let's say you want to leave your home to your children, but you also want to provide for your grandchildren's education. You could set up a trust that allows your children to live in the home for their lifetime, but upon their death, the home would be sold and the proceeds would be used to fund educational trusts for your grandchildren.

The third step is to communicate your plan with your loved ones. This includes having conversations with your family about your values, beliefs, and traditions, as well as your plan for your assets. It's important to involve your loved ones in the planning process so that they understand your wishes and can carry out your plan after you're gone.

For example, let's say you have a collection of art that you want to donate to a museum after your death. You should communicate this with your family members, so they know your wishes and can ensure that your collection is donated as you intended.

The fourth step is to review and update your plan regularly. This includes reviewing your will, trust, or other legal documents, as well as ensuring that your assets are properly titled. It's also important to review and update your plan as your values, beliefs, and goals change over time.

For example, let's say you've set up a trust to provide for your grandchildren's education, but one of them decides to pursue a career in the military instead. You would want to review and update the trust to ensure that it still aligns with your goals and values and that it's providing for your grandchildren as you intended.

In conclusion, legacy planning is the process of creating a plan to ensure that your assets and values are passed on to future generations in a way that aligns with your goals and values. It's important to understand your values and goals, create a plan for your assets, communicate your plan with your loved ones and review and update your plan regularly. By following these steps and making smart decisions, you can create a lasting legacy that aligns with your values and goals, and that will be passed on to future generations.

How to create a family mission statement

A family mission statement is a statement that defines the values, beliefs, and purpose of a family. It serves as a guide for decision making and helps to align the actions of family members with the family's shared values and goals. In this chapter, we will explore how to create a family mission statement and provide detailed examples of how to put this concept into practice.

The first step in creating a family mission statement is to gather input from all family members. This includes having open and honest discussions about the values, beliefs, and goals that are important to each member of the family. It's important to involve all family members in the process to ensure that the mission statement reflects the shared values and goals of the entire family.

For example, you could schedule a family meeting where each member is given the opportunity to share their thoughts on what they believe is important for the family and what they would like to see the family's mission statement to reflect.

The second step is to identify common themes and values. Once input has been gathered from all family members, it's important to identify the common themes and values that emerged during the discussions. These themes and values will serve as the foundation for the family's mission statement.

For example, let's say your family values education, community service and respect for others, those values would be included in the family's mission statement.

The third step is to write the mission statement. The mission statement should be a clear and concise statement that encapsulates the family's shared values and goals. It's important to keep the mission statement simple and easy to understand, so that it's easy for all family members to remember and follow.

For example, a family mission statement could be: "Our family is dedicated to fostering a lifelong love of learning, serving our community, and treating others with kindness and respect."

The fourth step is to share the mission statement with all family members and make it visible in your home. This could be hanging in a family room or on the refrigerator, it's important to make the mission statement visible, so that it serves as a constant reminder of the family's shared values and goals. Also, it's important to regularly review and discuss the mission statement as a family to ensure that it still aligns with the family's values and goals.

For example, you could schedule a family meeting every six months to review the mission statement and discuss how the family is living up to it and if any changes need to be made.

In conclusion, creating a family mission statement is an important step in aligning the actions of family members with the family's shared values and goals. It's important to gather input from all family members, identify common themes and values, write a clear and concise mission statement, share it with all family members and make it visible in your home and regularly review it. By following these steps and creating a shared mission statement, families can work together to achieve their shared goals and values, and create a stronger and more united family.

How to teach your children about money

Teaching children about money is an important step in helping them develop the skills and knowledge they need to make sound financial decisions in the future. In this chapter, we will explore how to teach your children about money and provide detailed examples of how to put this concept into practice.

The first step in teaching children about money is to start early. Children as young as three or four years old can begin to understand basic concepts like saving and spending. Starting early gives children a foundation of knowledge and skills that they can build on as they grow older.

For example, you could give your child a piggy bank and encourage them to save their allowance or money they receive as gifts. As they save, you could help them understand how their money is growing and the importance of saving for future purchases.

The second step is to lead by example. Children learn by example, so it's important to model good financial habits in your own behavior. This includes things like budgeting, saving, and spending wisely.

For example, you could involve your children in the budgeting process, showing them how you allocate your income for expenses and savings, and explaining the reasoning behind your decisions.

The third step is to use age-appropriate language and concepts. It's important to explain financial concepts in terms that children can understand. This includes using simple terms and concrete examples to help them grasp abstract concepts.

For example, you could use the example of a toy they want to buy, explain the cost, and help them understand the value of the money they have and the concept of earning more to buy the toy they want.

The fourth step is to give children opportunities to practice making financial decisions. This includes things like allowing them to make small purchases, giving them an allowance, or involving them in family financial decisions.

For example, you could give your child a small allowance and encourage them to save some, spend some, and give some to charity. You could also involve them in family financial decisions, such as choosing a family vacation destination or a purchase for the household.

The fifth step is to continue the conversation. Teaching children about money is an ongoing process, and it's important to continue the conversation as they grow older. This includes discussing financial topics as they arise and answering their questions as they come up.

For example, when your child is a teenager and starting to think about college or a first job, you could discuss the costs associated with those events and how they can plan and save for them.

In conclusion, teaching children about money is an important step in helping them develop the skills and knowledge they need to make sound financial decisions in the future. It's important to start early, lead by example, use age-appropriate language and concepts, give children opportunities to practice making financial decisions, continue the conversation and involve them in family financial decisions. By following these steps and creating an open and ongoing dialogue about money, you can help your children develop the financial literacy and decision-making skills they need to succeed in the future.

CHAPTER TWELVE

Conclusion Achieving Financial Success Through Wealthy Habits

The importance of developing and maintaining wealthy habits

Developing and maintaining wealthy habits is essential for achieving financial success and securing a comfortable future. Wealthy habits include things like budgeting, saving, investing, networking, and understanding the concept of financial independence. By implementing these habits, individuals can take control of their finances, grow their savings and build wealth over time. The key to success is to make these habits a part of your daily routine and to be consistent in your efforts. It's also important to remember that achieving financial success is a journey, and it's important to be patient, persistent and not to give up in the face of obstacles. By developing and maintaining wealthy habits, individuals can position themselves for a successful future and secure their financial independence.

How to continue learning about personal finance

Continuing to learn about personal finance is essential for achieving financial success and securing a comfortable future. Personal finance is a broad and ever-changing field, and it's important to stay informed and up-to-date with the latest information and best practices. There are many ways to continue learning about personal finance, including reading books and articles, attending seminars and workshops, and working with a financial advisor. Additionally, the use of online resources, such as personal finance blogs, podcasts, and online courses, can also be a great way to learn about personal finance and stay informed. By continuing to learn about personal finance, individuals can better understand how to manage their money and make informed financial decisions. This can help them to achieve financial success and secure a comfortable future. It is also important to note that personal finance is a life-long learning journey, so it's important to make learning about it a part of your daily routine and to be consistent in your efforts.

Strategies for staying motivated and on track

Staying motivated and on track is essential for achieving financial success and reaching your goals. Developing a solid plan and setting realistic, measurable goals is a great start, but it's also important to have strategies in place to keep yourself motivated and on track. Some strategies that can help include setting reminders and deadlines, tracking your progress, rewarding yourself for milestones, and surrounding yourself with supportive people. Additionally, it's important to stay positive and remind yourself of the reasons why you started and the benefits of achieving your goals. It's also important to be flexible and adapt your plan if necessary. Remember that setbacks and obstacles are a normal part of the journey, and it's important to not to give up on your goals. By staying motivated and on track, you can achieve your financial goals and secure a comfortable future.

Endnotes

1. "The Millionaire Mind," by Thomas J. Stanley
2. "Rich Dad Poor Dad," by Robert Kiyosaki
3. "The Total Money Makeover," by Dave Ramsey
4. "The Simple Path to Wealth," by JL Collins
5. "The Intelligent Investor," by Benjamin Graham
6. "The 4-Hour Work Week," by Timothy Ferriss
7. "Your Money or Your Life," by Vicki Robin and Joe Dominguez
8. "The Science of Getting Rich," by Wallace D. Wattles
9. "The Wealth of Nations," by Adam Smith
10. "The Power of Habit," by Charles Duhigg
11. "The Compound Effect," by Darren Hardy
12. "The Automatic Millionaire," by David Bach
13. "Smart Women Finish Rich," by David Bach
14. "Mastering the Game of Money," by T. Harv Eker
15. "The One Thing," by Gary Keller and Jay Papasan

These books and authors have been instrumental in shaping the ideas and concepts presented in this book. They have provided valuable insights and perspectives on wealth-building, personal finance, and financial success. I highly recommend them to anyone interested in further exploring the topics covered in this book.